LAND TITLES

LAND TITLES
REGISTRATION IN CANADA & THE U.S.A.

RICHARD H. STEACY

Real Estate Press, *Willowdale, Ontario*

Design: Brant Cowie/Artplus

Published by: REAL ESTATE PRESS
P.O. Box 222, Willowdale, Ontario, Canada
Canada's most exclusive real estate publishing house.

THIS BOOK was NOT published with any assistance from the Canada Council, or any Government loans or grants. It was published through the medium of a loan from the Canadian Imperial Bank of Commerce.

Printed and bound in Canada by The Bryant Press Limited, Toronto.

ISBN 0-9690470-1-0

CONTENTS

ACKNOWLEDGEMENT

G RATEFUL acknowledgement is expressed to the Government of the State of South Australia for its authority to publish the Act contained herein, the exact authority being: "It is a copy of the South Australian Real Property Act, 1858, republished by Mr. R. H. Steacy with the permission of the South Australian Government".

Acknowledgement and thanks is expressed to the following for their advice concerning registration of real property in Canada: MR. G. A. McINTYRE, Administrator, Government of the Yukon Territory, MR. F. G. SMITH, Q.C., Associate Director, Department of Public Services, Government of the Northwest Territories, MR. J. V. DiCASTRI, Director, Legal Services, Department of the Attorney General, British Columbia, MR. E. F. GA-MACHE, Registrar, North Alberta Land Registration District, MR. C. W. TRUSCOTT, Master of Titles, Saskatchewan, THE DEPUTY DISTRICT REGISTRAR, Department of the Attorney-General, Manitoba, MR. GOR-DON F. GREGORY, Deputy Minister, Department of Justice, New Brunswick, MR. INNIS G. MacLEOD, Deputy Attorney General, Nova Scotia, MR. J. W. MACNUTT, Legislative Counsel, Department of Justice, Prince Edward Island, THE HONOURABLE MR. I. ALEX HICKMAN, Minister of Justice, Government of Newfoundland and Labrador.

For advice on the Torrens system in the United States of America, many thanks to MR. DAVID M. deWILDE, Associate General Counsel, Department of Housing and Urban Development, Washington, D.C.

FOREWORD

Subsequent to the publication of my best selling *Canadian Real Estate: How To Make It Pay* many requests have come to my attention seeking additional information about "Land Titles".

The Registrar General of Deeds, Adelaide, South Australia, very kindly photographed the original Act for me, which is herewith published for the first time in Canada.

The "Torrens" or Land Titles System has been described as South Australia's greatest export.

Land registration systems are very ancient, and probably go back to Babylon. They were common in medieval Europe. The pattern for the earliest Australian systems were registers of deeds introduced in some English counties in the time of Queen Anne. But before the middle of the last century there was no system of land registration anywhere in the world which included all the desirable features of the "Torrens" system. It spread to North America in the 1880's, and a similar system was taken up by Germany and other European countries, by the French North African and other Mediterranean colonies, and by most of the British colonies and dependencies throughout the world. A "Torrens" system lay comparatively dormant in England from 1862 to 1925, when it became vitalised and is now flourishing.

The system removes all risk from defective deeds by enacting that the ownership of the person whose name shows in the register book shall be paramount. Registration makes his ownership conclusive. It cannot be forfeited. A person deprived of land through the operation of the system does not suffer loss, and if he is the victim of fraud he can recover possession of his land. If an innocent third party has become registered as proprietor, the victim can proceed against the wrongdoer, not for land, but for pecuniary damages, as the third party's title will be indefeasible. If that action fails, the victim can recover compensation from the Government.

Compared to registry office systems, land titles transfers have no complicated covenants as in deeds. The whole title, and everything it is subject to, is all on one page. Long descriptions are not required—by using Reference Plans short descriptions are used. Land Titles save a great deal of time in "searching title" since it is all on one page.

There can be no adverse possession under Land Titles.

For all those interested in the subject of real property, here is some fascinating reading from the pages of history, and brief summaries of Land Titles as it applies to Canada and the U.S.A.

Richard H. Steacy
P.O. Box 222,
Willowdale, Ontario, Canada.

SIR ROBERT RICHARD TORRENS

I N July, 1958, the State of South Australia honoured the memory and work
of a man who was convicted in Adelaide's Criminal Court—who caused
a French warship to be sent to Adelaide and cost the British Government thousands of pounds—who publicly thrashed a newspaper editor in
Hindley Street, Adelaide, and who changed the conveyancing laws in South
Australia and many other parts of the world.

July 1st, 1958, was the centenary of the South Australia Real Property Act, and honour was done to its author, Sir Robert Richard Torrens,
former Premier of South Australia, Collector of Customs, and Registrar-
General of Deeds.

One of the most controversial figures in South Australia history,
Torrens was both vilified and eulogised by the Adelaide press, politicians,
and the legal fraternity of the time.

The son of Colonel Torrens, chairman of the Board of Commissioners
responsible for the establishment of the colony of South Australia, Sir
Robert Torrens, as a clerk at the Customs House, London, was trained for a
business career. He became Collector of Customs on his arrival in Adelaide
in 1840.

Torrens soon came to grips with the authorities, and Governor Grey
on several occasions criticized him for his neglect, and deplored the fact that
he had not received from him "that cheerful acquiescence, in my view, which
I have received from other Government officers".

Torrens made his presence felt in Adelaide 12 months after his
appointment as Collector of Customs by his dramatic and colourful seizure
of the French barque Ville de Bordeaux.

Not satisfied with the ship's papers when he went aboard as she was
anchored in the gulf, he ordered the captain to put in to Port Adelaide. But
after he had returned to port, the barque, which was to have loaded 1,000
sheep and other cargo, prepared to leave.

Torrens, with a hastily gathered crew, manned an old paddle steamer, which promptly broke down. So, amid the jeers and cheers of a large crowd that had gathered on the waterfront, the crew stood on the paddles and worked them with their feet. The ship finally made the gulf, but after a fruitless search Torrens and his crew returned to find the barque in port, the crew having disobeyed the captain.

Adelaide's newspapers, already hostile to Torrens, made the most of this episode, alleging wrongful interference with the rights of a foreign power. Finally, a French warship, with the owner of the barque on board, arrived at Port Adelaide to investigate the affair. Although a court action held the barque to be at fault, the British Government paid £4,000 to the barque's owner as compensation.

But Torrens was correct in his suspicions of the ship, which was subsequently found to have been involved in various frauds. The Ville de Bordeaux remained at Port Adelaide, and was finally broken up.

Bitter attacks on Torrens by a section of the press continued, and eventually a Mr. Cassell was sent out from England to investigate the administration of his department. During the investigation, Torrens and his senior clerk, a Mr. Watson, made allegations against each other. Cassell supported Torrens, who suspended Watson.

The Adelaide "Register" published a story that Cassell was staying with Torrens, and that Watson had no chance of an impartial hearing. This so incensed Torrens that on meeting the editor, a Mr. George Stevenson, in Hindley street, he thrashed him with a walking stick. In its issue of March 14, 1849, the "Register" said: "So, we suppose in a day or two this colony will furnish the edifying spectacle of the Collector of Customs and a magistrate of the territory, standing in the dock as a felon".

There was some delay in the prosecution, and then Torrens came before the court, charged with having feloniously wounded Stevenson with intent to "maim, disfigure, disable, and do some grievous bodily harm". He was convicted for common assault. Torrens then sued Stevenson for libel, and was awarded a farthing damages.

When South Australia was granted responsible Government, in 1856, Torrens was elected as one of the members for Adelaide, and became Treasurer. In 1857 he formed a Ministry himself, but was Premier for only a month.

So much property was passing so quickly to so many new settlers in the early days of South Australia that the old English conveyancing laws could not cope with the situation. Bitter agitation among the settlers led to the formation of an active committee, in an endeavour to evolve a more simple, secure, and less costly method of obtaining titles to property.

Torrens wrote to the Governor, intimating his intention to suggest a Bill for amending the conveyancing laws. It was finally passed by Parliament.

In June, 1858, Torrens received the following letter from the South Australia Chief Secretary: "And the circumstances of your having originated the Act and been its principal supporter and promoter in Parliament, indicating you as the person most qualified, I have the honour, by direction of the Governor-in-Chief, to offer you the position of Registrar-General, at £1,000 per annum".

Torrens accepted the position, and resigned his seat in Parliament. But after the Act was passed, he was vilified by the press and legal profession. In their opposition to the Act, the lawyers adopted every device possible to render the measure ineffective—they advised their clients not to deal with any land which was under the Act.

Even the Bench showed a very critical attitude to the Act, years after Torrens had won the battle. In 1874, Mr. Justice Gwynne said of certain sections: "I would countenance this simple system (if anything so crude, so ill-conceived, clumsily executed, and unscientific, can be called a system) and accept it with all its sins against the science of jurisprudence, contenting ourselves with the reflection that it is cheap and simple and sufficient for the general purposes of the colonists . . . . In my opinion the Real Property Act as it stands at present is a scandal on the legislation of the Colony".

There is no doubt that Torrens regarded the opposition as springing largely from mercenary motives, as in a letter to the Attorney-General of Queensland, who had asked for a copy of the Act, Torrens wrote: "I have struck out the clauses relating to the licensing of land brokers, a provision which was necessitated here by the persistent and unscrupulous hostility of the conveyancers, but which it is hoped may not be necessary where more liberal sentiments animate the Bench and Bar".

Within 16 years the principles of the South Australia Act were being used by all the Australian States and New Zealand. Later, it spread to many parts of the world (about 60 countries) and to several States of the U.S.A.

Before Torrens departed for England in 1862, he was given an address signed by 10,000 citizens of Adelaide, and in 1864 petitions were made to both Houses of Parliament, signed by 14,000 people, praying that his services be recognized.

He was elected to the House of Commons for Cambridge in 1865, and received the K.C.M.G. in 1872. He was advanced to the G.C.M.G. in 1884, the year of his death.

LAND TITLES REGISTRATION IN CANADA

THE YUKON
TERRITORY:

The Canada Land Titles Act (Revised Statutes of Canada 1970, Chapter L-4) applies to the Yukon Territory, and it is a Torrens system.

THE NORTHWEST
TERRITORIES:

The Northwest Territories land registration system is purely Torrens.

BRITISH COLUMBIA:

With the exception of certain Crown lands, and a very small percentage of complicated titles, all lands are under the Torrens system.

ALBERTA:

The Province of Alberta was part of the North West Territories and became subject to the Territories Real Property Act 1886, Statutes of Canada, Chapter 26. This Act appears to be the oldest Torrens act in Canada. It was followed by the Land Titles Act 1894, Statutes of Canada, Chapter 28.

When the Province of Alberta was formed by the Alberta Act 1905, Statutes of Canada, Chapter 3, it took over the Torrens offices created by the Territories Real Property Act 1886, and the two Torrens Land Titles offices in Calgary and Edmonton.

Alberta passed its own Land Titles Act by 1906 Statutes of Alberta, Chapter 24.

Any land conveyed or granted prior to 1886 has been completely brought under the Torrens system. At the present time 100% of the land in Alberta is under the Torrens system.

SASKATCHEWAN:

All land in Saskatchewan is based on the Torrens system. This does not mean that all land in Saskatchewan has been brought under the Land Titles Act so that there is a certificate of title for all Saskatchewan land, but means that if any land in Saskatchewan is ever dealt with, it will be brought under the Act upon the registration of any transfer or grant from the Crown, etc.

About one-half of the land in Saskatchewan has been brought under the Land Titles Act, and approximately one-half is still owned by Her Majesty the Queen in the Right of Saskatchewan.

MANITOBA:

No accurate survey of all of the Land Titles Offices in Manitoba has ever been made to determine the proportions of land area or land holdings as divided between the two registration systems. The estimate is that over 85% of the settled land area in the Province and perhaps 95% of individual land holdings are under the Torrens system.

ONTARIO:

The Land Titles Act governs all land granted in the north after 1887.

In the south, the introduction of the land titles system into specific areas has been left throughout most of the past to the initiative of local authorities—the councils of counties, towns and cities. This power to take the initiative has been shifted to the Provincial Government.

Once the system is introduced into an area, an owner may apply to have his land so registered.

The Ontario Law Reform Commission recorded a reasonable estimate has been made that there are about 2,200,000 parcels of land in Ontario, of which 15% are governed by the land titles system.

QUEBEC:

No reference.

NEW BRUNSWICK:
NOVA SCOTIA:
PRINCE EDWARD ISLAND:

The Land Registry and Information Service, a project created by the Council of Maritime Premiers, is presently at work on a land survey and primary work leading to a land titles system. This project is jointly funded by the Federal and Provincial Governments, and is scheduled to accomplish a land titles registration in the three provinces over the next ten years.

NEWFOUNDLAND:

Studies are being conducted into a Federal-Provincial programme which may be available to Newfoundland. If implemented, it will probably result in the establishment of a satisfactory Land Titles system.

LAND TITLES REGISTRATION IN THE U.S.A.

THE United States Department of Housing and Urban Development conducted research on Torrens in connection with its Report on Mortgage Settlement Costs. The following brief history of Torrens in the United States is from the report.

Because of the complexities of determining a clear, transferable title under the prevailing recording act system, various reforms have been suggested which would eliminate the need for repeated searches and title examinations. The more significant of these proposals stem from a suggestion made in 1857 by Sir Robert Torrens, an Australian official, that the sovereign register and certify condition of title.

Although statutes vary, the following description applies to the most common registration system. It operates through a Bureau of Registration. Land transactions are registered and recorded in this office. Before registry, the title is fully investigated by the Registrar, who receives from the owner all the documentary evidence of title, description of boundary, etc. When the Registrar is satisfied that the title is perfect, he files all the old title papers and issues to the holder a certificate of ownership—a duplicate of which is filed in the Registrar's office. Written on the face of the certificate are all encumbrances on the property. If the estate is vested in fee simple, the title is known as "absolute" and the certificate is called an absolute certificate. Otherwise the title is referred to as "possessory".

If the absolute title is subject to reversions, then the Registrar will except from the effect of registration any estate right or interest arising before the specified date or conditions named. All the exceptions are entered in the register and noted on the certificate, which is then called a "qualified" certificate. The holder of a possessory title may obtain an absolute certificate upon giving such evidence of title as may be required.

Once completed, the examination and registration of title does not have to be repeated. The transfer of the certificate with accompanying entry in the Registrar's records completes the transfer of the grantor's interest in the land. Some statutes establish a cut-off date after which a title cannot be challenged (except for reasons of fraud). Should any person suffer loss through an undiscovered claim, misdescription, omission or any other error on the certificate, his loss would be indemnified by an insurance fund created for that purpose. Funds for the insurance pool are provided by the imposition of a tax—usually one quarter of one per cent of the value of the land at the time the first title registration certificate is issued for the parcel. The Registrar has sole control over dispensations made from the fund. Fees for title registration are minimal and the risk involved in accepting title is virtually eliminated.

The system has several advantages and is in much use throughout the world outside of the United States. The National Conference of Commissioners on Uniform Legislation drafted and approved a Uniform Land Registration Act in 1916 based on the Torrens principle.

Unfortunately for the Torrens movement, it made a poorly timed entrance upon the American scene. In the late 1800's America was too concerned with westward expansion to give Torrens a fair test. There were several factors which inhibited the universal acceptance of registration in America. The first was the inability to centralize pro-Torrens sentiment and make certification obligatory throughout the country. Secondly, although there was much criticism of the recording system at the time, anti-Torrens groups were politically powerful and able to appeal to the new American nationalism in order to defeat the adoption of a "foreign" system. Many opponents of registration attacked it as foreign intervention in American domestic affairs and contended that it had been introduced into Australia to enable the authorities to exercise control over the criminal elements who had been forced to migrate there.

Several peculiarly American problems operated against general American acceptance of land registration. At that time, there was little or no trained civil service at the local levels able to handle the details of title registration and certification. A system of registered titles presupposed accurate maps. At the time, these simply did not exist in many parts of the country.

For Torrens to be effective the accuracy of the certificate had to be backed by a larger fund than could be collected from fees deposited at the time of initial registration. Legislatures were loath to fund registry offices which, at that time, were often staffed by political appointees.

Most practicing real estate attorneys and legal academicians believe that the utilization of the Torrens system is not likely to expand in this country, because established interests would resist the change necessitated by its use.

Twelve states currently have such statutes on their books:
COLORADO, Rev. Stat. Amm. Ch. 118, Act 10 (1953)
GEORGIA, Code Amm. Tit. 60 (1937)
HAWAII, Rev. Laws Ch. 342 (1955)
ILLINOIS, Rev. Stat. Ch. 30 #45-152 (1961)
MASSACHUSETTS, Amm. Laws Ch. 185 (1955)
MINNESOTA, Stat. Amm. Ch. 508 (1947)
NEW YORK, Real Prop. Law #370-435
NORTH CAROLINA, Gen. Stat. Ch. 43 (1960)
OHIO, Rev. Code Ch. 5309, 5310 (1953)
OREGON, Rev. Stat. Ch. 94 (1961)
VIRGINIA, Acts Ch. 62 (1916)
WASHINGTON, Rev. Code Ch. 65.12 (1961)

The following states have had Torrens statutes, which have been repealed:

CALIFORNIA	(1897)
MISSISSIPPI	(1914)
NEBRASKA	(1915)
SOUTH CAROLINA	(1916)
TENNESSEE	(1917)
NORTH DAKOTA	(1917)
SOUTH DAKOTA	(1917)
UTAH	(1917)

VICTORIÆ REGINÆ No. 15

An Act to simplify the Laws relating to the transfer and encumbrance of freehold and other interests in Land.

[Assented to, 27th January, 1858.]

Preamble.

WHEREAS the inhabitants of the Province of South Australia are subjected to losses, heavy costs, and much perplexity, by reason that the laws relating to the transfer and encumbrance of freehold and other interests in land are complex, cumbrous, and unsuited to the requirements of the said inhabitants, it is therefore expedient to amend the said laws—Be it Enacted, by the Governor-in-Chief, of the said Province, with the advice and consent of the Legislative Council and House of Assembly of the said Province, in this present Parliament assembled, as follows:

Repeal of previous Acts.

1. All Laws, Statutes, Acts, Ordinances, rules, regulations, and practice whatsoever, relating to freehold and other interests in land, so far as inconsistent with the provisions of this Act, are hereby repealed, so far as regards their application to land under the provisions of this Act, or the bringing of land under the operation of this Act.

Short title.

2. This Act may be cited for all purposes as the "Real Property Act."

Interpretation of certain terms.

3. In the construction, and for the purposes of this Act, and in all instruments purporting to be made or executed thereunder (if not inconsistent with the context and subject matter), the following terms shall have the respective meanings hereinafter assigned to them, that is to say—

The word "Land" shall extend to and include messuages, tenements, and hereditaments, corporeal and incorporeal, of every kind and description, (whether of a greater or less description than life estates, and whether at law or in equity), together with all paths, passages, ways, waters, water-courses, liberties, privileges, easements, plantations, gardens, mines, minerals, and quarries, and all trees and timber thereon or thereunder, lying or being, unless the same are specially excepted:

"Grant" shall mean the land grant of any land of the Crown by any Resident Commissioner or Governor of the said Province, to any person or persons:

"Proprietor" shall mean any person seised or possessed of any estate at law or in equity, in possession, in futurity, or expectancy, whether a life estate, or of a greater or less description than a life estate, in any land.

"Transfer" shall mean the execution of every instrument, and the performance of every formality, including registration, required by this Act; to give validity to the passing, either of the whole of the proprietor's interest in land, or of any less estate therein:

"Memorandum of Sale" shall mean the instrument executed by the person having estate or interest in land under the operation of this Act, for the purpose of transferring such estate and interest in form of the Schedule hereto annexed, marked B:

"Transmission" shall mean the acquirement of title to or interest in lands, consequent on the will, intestacy, bankruptcy, insolvency, or marriage of a proprietor:

"Certificate of Title" shall mean the instrument executed by the Registrar-General, in form A of the Schedule hereto annexed, duplicate of which constitutes a separate page in the register book, vesting the fee simple, or any less estate (as the case may be), in land brought under the operation of this Act:

"Mortgage" shall be applicable to every charge on, or interest in land, created merely for securing a loan:

"Mortgagor" shall mean the borrower of money on the security of any estate or interest in land under the operation of this Act:

"Mortgagee" shall mean the lender of money upon the security of any estate or interest in land under the operation of this Act:

"Bill of Mortgage" shall mean the instrument in form of the Schedule hereto annexed, marked D, required under this Act to be executed by the intending mortgagor, with a view to creating such mortgage as last aforesaid:

"Encumbrance" and "Assignment" shall mean the execution by a person of every necessary or suitable instrument, and the performance of every formality, including registration, required by this Act, for assigning, surrendering, or otherwise transferring land of which such person is possessed, either for the whole estate of the person so possessed or for any less estate, in order to render such land available for securing the payment of any annuity or dower, or for the payment of any sum of money either absolutely or subject to conditions, restrictions, or contingencies; including also the execution, by the Registrar-General, of every instrument, and the performance by him of every formality required by this Act to give validity to such encumbrance or assignment:

"Encumbrancer" shall mean the person, not being a mortgagor, who shall have assigned any estate or interest in land under the operation of this Act for the purpose of securing any annuity, dower, or sum of money:

"Encumbrancee" shall mean the person, not being a mortgagee, to whom or for whose benefit any estate or interest in land under the provisions of this Act shall have been encumbered or assigned:

"Bill of Encumbrance" or "Bill of Trust" shall mean the instrument creating such encumbrance or assignment executed by the person having estate or interest in land under the operation of this Act in form of one or other of the Schedules hereto annexed, marked respectively E or F:

"Estate in Fee Simple" shall mean the absolute property in land, such as is originally vested by a "Grant" in the meaning of this Act:

"Registration Abstract" shall mean the instrument under the hand and seal of the Registrar-General, executed in form of the Schedule hereto marked H, or in words to the like effect, available in lieu of the Register Book, for the purpose of enabling a person to mortgage or to sell, in places without the limits of the said Province, land under the operation of this Act whereof he may be seised as proprietor:

"Lunatic" shall mean any person who shall be found to be a lunatic upon inquiry by the Supreme Court, or by any Judge thereof, or upon a Commission of Inquiry issuing out of the Supreme Court in the nature of a writ *de lunatico inquirendo*:

The expression "Person of Unsound Mind" shall mean any person not an infant, who, not having been found to be a lunatic, shall be incapable, from infirmity of mind, to manage his own affairs:

"Consular Officer" shall include Consul-General, Consul, and Vice-Consul, and any person for the time being discharging the duties of Consul-General, Consul, or Vice-Consul:

"Registrar-General" shall mean the Registrar-General, or other officer duly authorized or appointed to carry out the provisions of this Act, or any person duly authorized as Deputy of such Registrar-General, or to act on his behalf in respect to this Act:

"Instrument" shall mean and include any land grant, certificate of title, or other document in writing, relating to the transfer, encumbrance, or other dealing with land:

"Register Book" shall mean the book hereinafter directed to be kept for the purpose of recording therein, in order, grants and certificates of titles issued, and the execution of instruments affecting land under the operation of this Act:

"Person," used and referred to in the masculine gender, shall include a female as well as a male, and shall include a body corporate:

The naming any person as proprietor, vendor, mortgagor, mortgagee, encumbrancer, encumbrancee, lessor or lessee, or as trustee, or as seised of or having any estate or interest in any land, shall be deemed to include the heirs, executors, administrators, and assigns of such person:

And, generally, unless the contrary shall appear from the context, every word importing the singular number only shall extend to several persons or things, and every word importing the plural number shall apply to one person or thing, and every word importing the masculine gender only shall extend to a female.

4. The department of the Registrar-General shall be the department to undertake the general superintendence of matters relating to the transfer, transmission, sale, mortgage, and encumbrancing of all land under the operation of this Act, and the releasing of such land from any mortgage or encumbrance, and shall be authorized to carry into execution the provisions of this Act, and of any Acts to amend or extend the provisions of this Act in force for the time being.

Functions of the Registrar-General and his department.

5. All documents whether purporting to be issued or written by or under the directions of the Registrar-General, and purporting either to be sealed with his seal or signed by him, or by one of his deputies shall be received in evidence, and shall be deemed to be issued or written by or under the direction of the Registrar-General without further proof unless the contrary be shown.

Certificates and documents purporting to be signed and sealed in a given manner to be received as evidence.

6. The Registrar-General may, with the consent of the Governor, for the purposes of carrying into effect the provisions contained in this Act, give

Registrar-General may make rules.

such instructions as to the manner of making entries in the register book, as to the execution and attestation of instruments as to any evidence to be required for identifying any person, and generally as to any act or thing to be done in pursuance of this Act, as he may think fit.

14

Registrar-General, with sanction of Governor, to issue forms of instruments, &c.

7. The Registrar-General may, with the consent of the Governor of the said Province from time to time prepare and sanction forms of the various books, instruments, and papers required by this Act, and may with like sanction from time to time make such alterations therein as he deems requisite; and shall, before finally issuing or altering any such form, give such public notice thereof as he deems necessary in order to prevent inconvenience; and shall cause every such form to be sealed with such seal as aforesaid, or marked with some other distinguishing mark, and to be supplied at the General Registry Office free of charge, or at such moderate prices as he may from time to time fix, or may licence any person to print and sell the same; and every such instrument and paper as aforesaid shall be made in the form issued by the Registrar-General, and sanctioned by him as the proper form for the time being; and every such instrument or paper, if made in a form purporting to be a proper form, and to be sealed or marked as aforesaid, shall be taken to be made in the form hereby required, unless the contrary is proved.

Penalty for counterfeiting seal, fraudulently altering forms, and for not using forms issued by Registrar-General.

8. Every person who counterfeits, assists in counterfeiting, or procures to be counterfeited, such seal or other distinguishing mark as aforesaid, or who fraudulently alters, assists in fraudulently altering, or procures to be fraudulently altered, any form issued by the Registrar-General with the view of evading any of the provisions of this Act or any condition contained in such form, shall for each offence be deemed guilty of a misdemeanor, and shall incur a penalty not exceeding One Hundred Pounds; or may, at the discretion of the Court before whom such case may be tried, be imprisoned for any period not exceeding twelve calendar months; and every person who, in any case in which a form sanctioned by the Registrar-General is by this Act required to be used, uses without reasonable excuse any form not purporting to be so sanctioned, or who prints, sells, or uses any document purporting to be a form so sanctioned, knowing the same not to be so sanctioned for the time being, or not to have been prepared and issued by the Registrar-General, shall for each such offence incur a penalty not exceeding Ten Pounds.

Powers of Registrar.

9. The Registrar-General may exercise the following powers, that is to say—

(1.) He may require the proprietor or other person making application to have any land brought under the operation of this Act, or the proprietor, or mortgagee, or other person interested in any land under the operation of this Act, in respect of which any transfer, lease, mortgage, or other encumbrance, or any release from any mortgage or encumbrance, is about to be transacted, or in respect of which any transmission is about to be registered, or a registration abstract granted under this Act, to produce any land grant, certificate of title, conveyance, bill of sale, mortgage deed, lease, will, or any other instrument in his possession or within his control affecting such land or the title thereto:

To inspect documents.

(2.) He may summon any such proprietor, mortgagee, or other person as aforesaid to appear, and give any explanation respecting such land, or the instruments affecting the title thereto, and if, upon requisition duly made by the Registrar-General, such proprietor, mortgagee, or other person refuses or neglects to produce any such instrument, or to allow the same to be inspected, or refuses or neglects to give any explanation which he is hereinbefore required to give, or knowingly misleads or deceives any person hereinbefore authorized to demand any such explanation, he shall for each such offence incur a penalty not exceeding Twenty Pounds; and the Registrar-General, if the instrument or information so withheld appears to him material, shall not be bound to proceed with the bringing of such land under the operation of this Act, or with the registration of such mortgage or sale, or with the issuing of such powers of mortgage or sale as the case may be:

He may summon and examine witnesses.

(3.) He may administer oaths, or, in lieu of administering an oath, may require any person examined by him to make and subscribe a declaration of the truth of the statements made by him in his examination.

He may administer oaths.

10. It shall be lawful for the Governor, with the advice of the Executive Council, by warrant under his hand and the public seal of the said Province, to appoint two persons, not being legal practitioners, who, together with the Registrar-General, shall be Commissioners for investigating and dealing with claims for the bringing of land under the provisions of this Act, and from time to time with like advice and in like manner to remove any of such Commissioners so appointed from office, and to appoint another person in his place.

Appointment of Lands Titles Commissioners.

11. The style of such Commissioners shall be the "Lands Titles Commissioners." The Registrar-General shall receive a reasonable salary. The other

Style, remuneration, form of procedure.

Commissioners shall be remunerated by fees on applications referred to them for bringing lands under the operation of this Act as set forth in the Schedule hereto marked T. At meetings of the said Lands Titles Commissioners, two shall form a quorum, and the Registrar-General, if present, shall preside as Chairman.

Solicitors to be appointed.

12. It shall be lawful for the said Commissioners, subject to the approval of the Governor, to appoint two legal practitioners, at reasonable salaries, to be their solicitors and permanent counsel, and also, subject to the like approval, to dismiss and discharge such solicitors and to appoint others in their stead.

Land alienated after the first day of July, 1858, to be subject to provisions of this Act.

13. All land alienated from the Crown within the said Province, from and after the first day of July, one thousand eight hundred and fifty-eight, shall be subject to the provisions of this Act.

Lands granted prior to the day on which this Act comes into operation may be brought under the operation of this Act.

14. Land, in the said Province, the grants of which may have been signed prior to the day appointed for this Act to come into operation, (whether such land shall constitute the entire or part only of the land included in any grant), may, at the desire of the proprietor, be brought under the operation of this Act in the following manner, that is to say—The proprietor shall deliver to the Registrar-General an application in form of the Schedule, hereto annexed, marked I, or in words to the like effect, and shall at the same time deposit with the Registrar-General all instruments in his possession or under his control constituting or in any way affecting his title to such land, together with an abstract of title in which he shall set forth and describe every instrument constituting or in any way affecting his title to such land, with the names and, so far as shall be within his knowledge, the addresses of all persons, if any, seised or possessed of any estate or interest in such land at law or in equity, in possession or in futurity, or expectancy, whether a life estate or of a greater or less description than a life estate, and shall make and subscribe a declaration to the truth of such abstract; or if such applicant proprietor be the sole and only person having estate or interest in such land, then he shall make and subscribe a declaration to that effect.

When applicant proprietor is original grantee and no transactions have taken place.

15. If, upon receipt of such application, it shall appear to the satisfaction of the Registrar-General that the applicant proprietor is the original grantee of the land in respect to which application is made, and that such land has been granted on or subsequent to the nineteenth day of October, one thousand eight hundred and forty-two, and that no sale, mortgage, or other encumbrance transaction in any way affecting the title to such land has at any time been registered in the said Province, then, and in such case, the Registrar-General shall, once in each of two successive weeks, give public notice by advertisement in the *South Australian Government Gazette*, and in, at the least, one newspaper published in the City of Adelaide, in the said Province, that application has been made for the bringing of such land under the operation of this Act, which notice shall be in the form of the Schedule hereto annexed, marked J, or in words to the like effect; and the Registrar-General shall likewise cause copy of such notice to be posted in a conspicuous place in his office, and in such other public places as he may deem necessary; and in any such case if the Registrar-General shall not, within the space of two calendar months from the date of the latest of such advertisements as hereinbefore directed to be published, receive any caveat as hereinafter described, with respect to such land, it shall be lawful for him, by notice to that effect published in the *South Australian Government Gazette*, to bring such land under the operation of this Act.

16. If it shall appear to the satisfaction of the Registrar-General that the applicant proprietor is not the original grantee of the land included in such application, or that the said land was granted prior to the nineteenth day of October, one thousand eight hundred and forty-two, or that any transfer, transmission, mortgage, encumbrance, or beneficial interest, affecting the title to such land has been made, or has been registered in the said Province, or elsewhere, then and in such case the Registrar-General shall refer such application to the Lands Titles Commissioners for their consideration, and if it shall appear to the satisfaction of the said Commissioners that the title to the land included in such application has not been derived by transmission, and that every mortgage, encumbrance, or beneficial interest, affecting the title to the land so included has been released and satisfied, or if any such mortgage, encumbrance, or interest, remains unsatisfied, that the parties interested therein are also parties to such application, then, and in either such case, the said Commissioners shall make and subscribe a warrant addressed to the Registrar-General, in form of the Schedule hereto annexed marked K, or in words to the like effect, which warrant shall contain a direction to the Registrar-General to cause notice of such application to be advertised three several times in the *South Australian Government Gazette*, and in at least one newspaper published in the City of Adelaide, and shall further limit and appoint a time, not less than one month nor more than twelve months from the date of the latest of such advertisements, upon or after the expiration of which, it shall be lawful for the Registrar-General,

When applicant proprietor is not original grantee and mortgages are satisfied or parties thereto are also parties to application and no transmissions have taken place.

When evidence of title is not clear, or transmissions have taken place, or parties interested in unsatisfied mortgages are not parties to the application.

unless he shall in the interval have received a caveat as hereinafter described, to bring such land under the operation of this Act; but if it shall appear to the satisfaction of the said Commissioners that the title to the land included in such application has been derived by transmission, or that any parties interested in any unsatisfied mortgage or encumbrance affecting the title to such land, or any other party, beneficially interested therein, are not parties to such application, or that the evidence of title set forth by such applicant proprietor is imperfect, it shall be lawful for such Commissioners to direct the Registrar-General to reject such application altogether, or, at their discretion, by warrant under their hand, in form of the Schedule hereto annexed marked K, or in words to the like effect, to direct the Registrar-General to cause notice of such application to be published in the *South Australian Government Gazette*, and in the *London Gazette* and in the *Official Gazettes* of each of the Colonies of New South Wales, Victoria, Tasmania, and New Zealand, or in any one or more of such *Gazettes*, and the said Commissioners shall in such warrant specify the number of times, and at what intervals, such advertisement shall be published in each or any of such *Gazettes*, and shall also limit and appoint a time, not less than two months nor more than three years from the date of the latest of such advertisements, upon or after the expiration of which, it shall be lawful for the Registrar-General, unless he shall in the interval have received a caveat as hereinafter described, to bring such land under the operation of this Act.

Notice to parties having any registered interest or title.

17.   The Registrar-General, upon receipt of any such warrant as is hereinbefore for either case respectively directed to be issued under the hand of such Commissioners, shall cause notice to be published in such manner as in such warrant may be directed, that application had been made for bringing the land referred to in such warrant under the operation of this Act, and shall also cause copy of such notice to be posted in a conspicuous place in his office, and in such other public places as he may deem necessary; and the Registrar-General shall likewise forward through the post office copy of such notice, addressed to each former proprietor, mortgagee, or other person who may then, or at any previous time, have had or held any legal or equitable title, claim, or encumbrance, to or upon such land, as far as his knowledge of the facts of the case, and of the names and addresses of such persons may enable him, and if the Registrar-General shall not, within the time for that purpose limited and appointed in any such warrant, receive any caveat as hereinafter described, it shall be lawful for him, by notice published in the *South Australian Government Gazette*, to bring the land referred to or described in such warrant under the operation of this Act.

18. It shall be lawful for any person having or claiming an interest in any land so advertised as aforesaid, or for the attorney of any person having or claiming interest therein, within the time hereinbefore limited and appointed, or that may by warrant as aforesaid, under the hands of the Lands Titles Commissioners, be for that purpose limited and appointed, to lodge a caveat with the Registrar-General forbidding the bringing of such land under the operation of this Act, which caveat shall be in the form of the Schedule hereto annexed, marked L, or as near thereto as circumstances permit, and shall particularize the estate, interest, lien, or charge, claimed by the person lodging the same; and if such claim is made under any instruments other than those set forth in the abstract deposited by the applicant proprietor, the person lodging such caveat shall deliver a full and complete abstract of his title, which shall contain the same matters, and be subject to the same regulations as are hereinbefore prescribed for the case of an abstract deposited by the applicant proprietor.

19. The Registrar-General, upon receipt of any such caveat within the time for either case limited as aforesaid, shall notify the same to such applicant proprietor, and shall suspend further action in the matter, and the lands in respect of which such caveat may have been lodged shall not be brought under the operation of this Act until such caveat shall have been withdrawn or shall have lapsed from any of the causes hereinafter provided, or until a decision shall have been obtained from the Court having jurisdiction in the matter.

20. After the expiration of three calendar months from the date thereof, every caveat shall be deemed to have lapsed unless the person by whom or on whose behalf the same was lodged shall, within that time, have taken proceedings to establish his title to the estate, interest, lien, or charge therein specified, and every person who shall fail to show probable cause for lodging such caveat to the satisfaction of the Judge before whom any prosecution may in such case be instituted, shall forfeit and pay a penalty not exceeding One Hundred Pounds.

21. If, upon the application of any proprietor to have land, of which he is seised, brought under the operation of this Act, the Registrar-General shall refuse so to do, or if such applicant proprietor shall be dissatisfied with the direction upon his application, given by the Lands Titles Commissioners as hereinbefore provided it shall be lawful for such applicant proprietor to require the Registrar-General to set forth in writing, under his hand, his objections to the title of such applicant proprietor or the grounds upon which such direction was given, and such applicant proprietor may, if he think fit, at his own costs, summons such Registrar-General to appear before the Supreme Court to substantiate and uphold his objections to such title, such summons to be issued at the request of such applicant proprietor, or his solicitor, under the hand of a Judge of the said Court, and served upon such Registrar-General six clear days, at least, before the day appointed for the hearing of such objections, and such objections shall be heard by the said Court upon motion; and upon such hearing the said Court shall, if any such objections be a question of fact, direct an issue to be tried to decide such fact; and it shall thereupon be lawful for the said Court to forbid the bringing of such land under the operation of this Act, or to order that such land may be brought under the same, after the expiration of such period of time, as the said Court shall think fit, not exceeding the period limited by any law, for the time being in force in the said Province, as the period within which actions of ejectment may be brought, and the Registrar-General shall obey such order.

Case may be argued by counsel; expense to be borne by applicant.

22. Upon any such motion as aforesaid, it shall be lawful for any person interested in any land touching or concerning the title to which such motion shall be made, and for the said Registrar-General by himself or his counsel, to argue the same before the said Court, in support of or objection to, the bringing of such land under the operation of this Act, and the Registrar-General, or his solicitor, shall have the right of reply; and all expenses attendant upon any of the matters or proceedings aforesaid, shall be borne and paid by the person requiring such land to be brought under the operation of this Act.

Form of notice for bringing land under operation of this Act.

23. Every notice for bringing land under the operation of this Act, hereinbefore directed to be published, shall be in the form of the Schedule hereto annexed, marked M, or in words to the like effect, and shall take effect and be valid to all intents from the date of the publication thereof.

Who entitled to bring land under Act, and receive certificate of title.

24. The person entitled to bring land under the operation of this Act, and to receive a certificate of title in respect of the same, shall be the person in whom the fee simple is vested, or if there be no person in whom the fee simple is vested, then the person so entitled shall be the person holding the greatest estate and interest in such land, not being a mortgagee thereof: Provided always, that no mortgagor shall be entitled to bring land under the operation of this Act, or to receive a certificate of title for the same, without the consent of his mortgagee, which consent may be endorsed on the form of application in manner hereinafter prescribed.

25. It shall be lawful for any proprietor, being an applicant to have land brought under the operation of this Act, to withdraw his application at any time prior to the issuing of such notice; and the Registrar-General shall, in such case, upon request in writing, signed by such applicant proprietor, return to him the abstract, and all instruments of title, deposited by such proprietor for the purpose of supporting his application.

Applicant proprietor may withdraw his application.

26. The Registrar-General shall not notice any caveat forbidding the bringing of land under the operation of this Act, if the party lodging the same claims only an estate or interest to take effect after the determination, or in defeasance of an estate tail, or forbids the bringing of such land under the operation of this Act, on the plea only of the absence of legal evidence that a former proprietor was in being and capable at the time when any power of attorney executed by such proprietor was exercised by his attorney in the selling or purchasing, or releasing of such land.

Caveats in certain cases not to bar the bringing of land under this Act.

27. Every grant, certificate of title, memorandum of sale, bill of mortgage, power of attorney, registration abstract, revocation order, bill of encumbrance, bill of trust, lease, or other instrument transferring or in any way affecting any estate or interest in land under the operation of this Act shall be in duplicate, and one original of every such instrument shall be filed in the Registry Office, and the other delivered to the proprietor or other person interested therein, or entitled thereto, and every instrument in this Act directed to be filed or bound up in the register book, being so filed or bound up shall be held to be "Registered by Deposit," in terms of an Act passed by the Governor and Legislative Council of the said Province on the ninth day of December, in the year of our Lord one thousand eight hundred and fifty-three, and in the seventeenth year of Her Majesty Queen Victoria, intituled "An Act to provide for the Deposit of Deeds, Agreements, Writings, and Assurances, Maps and Plans, relating to Hereditaments in the Province of South Australia, and for other purposes therein mentioned."

Grants and other instruments filed or bound up in register book deemed "Registered by Deposit."

28. The Registrar-General shall keep a book to be called the "Register Book of Real Property," and shall bind up therein the duplicates of all grants and of all certificates of title issued from and after the first day of July, one thousand eight hundred and fifty-eight, and shall open therein a separate page for each grant and certificate of title, and shall record thereon the

Registrar-General to keep register book.

particulars of all instruments affecting the land included under each such grant or certificate of title, distinct and apart.

Certificate of title to be issued when land is brought under the operation of this Act.

29. So soon as any land has been brought under the operation of this Act, the Registrar-General shall make out and deliver to the proprietor a certificate of title to the same in form hereinafter described, and every such certificate of title shall contain a reference to the original grant or other instrument evidencing title, which may have been deposited by such proprietor when making application in manner hereinbefore described, and the Registrar-General shall endorse on every such grant or instrument so surrendered a memorandum setting forth that the said grant or instrument had been surrendered by such proprietor in exchange for a certificate of title to such land pursuant to the provisions of this Act, with the date of such deposit; and if any grant or other instrument so deposited shall relate to or include any property, whether personal or real, other than the land included in such certificate of title, then the Registrar-General shall endorse on such grant or other instrument a memorandum setting forth that the said grant or instrument is cancelled in so far only as relates to the land included in such certificate of title, and shall return such grant or other instrument to such proprietor, otherwise he shall retain the same in his office.

Instruments of title if they include other property to be returned to applicant proprietor.

Certificate of title to be in duplicate, and to be bound up in register.

30. Every certificate of title made out by the Registrar-General shall be in duplicate, and in the form marked A in the Schedule hereto, and the Registrar-General shall note by endorsement thereon, and in such manner as to preserve their priority, the particulars of all unsatisfied mortgages or other encumbrances, and of every lease, rent, charge, or term of years, or outstanding estate whatsoever, affecting such land, which shall have been registered, or of which he may have notice, and shall cause one of such certificates of title to be bound up in the register book, and deliver the other to the proprietor entitled to the land described in such certificate, and every such certificate, duly authenticated under the hand and seal of the Registrar-General shall be received in all Courts of Justice as evidence of the particulars therein set forth and of their being entered in the register book in the manner set forth in such certificate.

Instruments not effectual until entry in registry book, or on registration abstract.

31. No instrument shall be effectual to pass any estate or interest in any land under the operation of this Act, or to render such land liable as security for the payment of money, but so soon as the Registrar-General shall have entered the particulars thereof in the book of registry, and made endorsement on such instrument as hereinafter directed to be made in each such case respectively, the estate or interest shall pass or, as the case may be, the land shall become liable to security in manner and subject to the conditions and contingencies set forth and specified in such instrument; and should two or more instruments executed by the same proprietor, and purporting to transfer or encumber the same estate or interest in any land, be at the same time presented to the Registrar-General for registration and endorsement, he shall register and endorse that instrument, under which the person claims property, who shall present to him the grant or certificate of title of such land for that purpose.

32. The Registrar-General shall not register any instrument purporting to transfer, or otherwise to deal with or affect any estate or interest in land under the operation of this Act, unless such instrument be in accordance with the provisions thereof.

Instruments not to be registered unless in accordance with prescribed forms.

33. Every certificate of title or entry in the register book shall be conclusive, and vest the estate and interests in the land therein mentioned in such manner and to such effect as shall be expressed in such certificate or entry valid to all intents, save and except as is hereinafter provided in the case of fraud or error.

Entry in register book conclusive.

34. Upon the first bringing of any land under the operation of this Act, and also upon the registering of the title to any land transmitted by will or intestacy, there shall be paid to the Registrar-General the sum of one farthing in the pound sterling on the value of the land so brought under the operation of this Act or so transmitted, and if such land be situated within the limits of any Corporation or District Council, the declaration of such applicant proprietor, or person entitled under such transmission, accompanied by the certificate of the Mayor or of the Chairman of such Corporation or District Council, setting forth the marketable value of such land at the time then being, and the amounts at which such land had been assessed at the assessment last before the bringing of such land under the operation of this Act, or last before such transmission, as the case may be, shall be received by the Registrar-General as sufficient evidence of the value of such land; and if such land be not situated within the limits of any Corporation or District Council, or being within such limits it shall not have been assessed, the oath or solemn affirmation of the applicant proprietor or of the party entitled under such transmission, made before the Registrar-General, or any Justice of the Peace, shall be received by such Registrar-General as evidence of the value of such land: Provided always that if the Registrar-

Per centage, Assurance Fund.

General shall not be satisfied as to the correctness of the value so declared or sworn to, it shall be lawful for him to require such proprietor or other person as aforesaid to produce a certificate of such value under the hand of a sworn appraiser, which certificate shall be received as conclusive evidence of such value for the purposes herein specified.

Assurance Fund to be invested in Government Securities.

35. All sums of money so received as aforesaid, shall be paid to the Treasurer of the said Province to constitute an Assurance Fund, out of which shall be made good the full amount awarded by any verdict or decree of Court to the rightful heir or proprietor of land under the operation of this Act as hereinafter provided, failing the recovery of such amount from the person who may by fraud, misrepresentation, or error, have become registered as proprietor of the same; and the said Treasurer may from time to time invest such sums in the South Australian Government Securities: Provided always that in case of deficiency in such Assurance Fund the full amount so awarded shall be made good to such rightful heir or proprietor out of the General Revenues of the said Province.

Deficiency to be made good out of General Revenue.

Transfer by sale.

36. When land under the operation of this Act is intended to be disposed of by sale, the vendor shall execute a memorandum of sale, in form of the Schedule hereto annexed marked B, or as near thereto as circumstances permit, which memorandum shall contain such description of the land intended to be transferred as is contained in the original grant, or in the certificate of title of such land, or such description as may be sufficient to identify that particular portion of land which it is intended to dispose of, and shall contain an accurate statement of the estate or interest of such vendor intended to be transferred, and a memorandum of all mortgages and other encumbrances affecting the same; and if such land be leased, the name and description of the lessee with a memorandum of the lease, and every such memorandum of sale shall be attested by a witness.

Registration of transfer.

37. Every memorandum of sale for the transfer of land under the operation of this Act, when duly executed, shall be produced to the Registrar-General, who shall thereupon enter in the register book, under the original entry respecting such land, the name, residence, and description of the vendor, or of each vendor if more than one; the name, residence, and description of the purchaser, or of each purchaser if more than one; the amount of the consideration money paid; the date of the memorandum of sale, and of its production, and such other particulars as the Registrar-General may deem necessary, and shall endorse on such memorandum of sale, and also on the

grant or certificate of title, the fact of such entry having been made, with the date and hour thereof, and shall sign each such endorsement and shall affix his seal to such memorandum of sale, and the particulars of every such memorandum of sale shall be entered in the register book in the order of the production thereof, and upon such entry being made by the Registrar-General, the land, or the estate or interest therein, as set forth and limited in such memorandum of sale as to be transferred, shall pass to and vest in the purchaser.

Memoranda of sale to be entered in the order of their production.

38. If the estate or interest in such land, so passed to and vested in such purchaser in manner aforesaid, shall be of a description less than a fee simple, the memorandum of sale so endorsed and authenticated, under the hand and seal of the Registrar-General, shall be received in any Court of Justice as sufficient evidence of the title of such purchaser to the estate or interest therein set forth and limited.

Memorandum of sale legal evidence.

39. If the memorandum of sale purports to transfer a full estate in fee simple in any land, the vendor shall at the same time deliver up the grant or certificate of title of such land, and the Registrar-General shall in such case endorse on such grant or certificate of title, a memorandum cancelling such grant or certificate of title, setting forth the day and hour on which such grant or certificate of title had been delivered up to him for that purpose, with the name, residence, and description of the vendor by whom the same was so given up, and the particulars of the transfer occasioning the surrender and cancelling of such grant or certificate of title.

Vendor to deliver up land grant or certificate of title.

Memorandum to be endorsed.

40. The Registrar-General shall thereupon make out a certificate of title of such land to the purchaser, referring therein to the original grant of such land, and to the memorandum of sale thereof, to such purchaser; and in case the vendor shall, by such memorandum of sale as aforesaid, have contracted to transfer the fee simple of part only of the land included under the grant or certificate of title so delivered up to be cancelled, then the Registrar-General shall make out a certificate of title to such proprietor of the unsold balance of such land so included as aforesaid.

Certificate of title to be issued to purchaser of estate in fee simple.

When part only is sold, new certificate for unsold portion to be issued to proprietor.

41. If any estate or interest in land under the operation of this Act, or any charge on such land, become transmitted in consequence of the death, or bankruptcy, or insolvency of any proprietor, or in consequence of the marriage settlement of any female proprietor, or by any lawful means other than by a transfer according to the provisions of this Act, such transmission

Declaration, in case of transmission by death, bankruptcy, or marriage.

shall be notified to the Registrar-General, by a declaration of the person to whom such estate or interest has come by transmission, made in the form marked N, in the Schedule hereto, and containing a statement describing the manner in which and the party to whom such estate or interest has come by transmission, and such declaration shall be made and subscribed if the declarant resides at or within ten miles of the General Registry Office, then in the presence of the Registrar-General; if beyond that distance, then in the presence of the Registrar-General or any Justice of the Peace; if the declarant resides in the United Kingdom of Great Britain and Ireland, or in any British Possession, other than the said Province, or in any foreign place, then in the presence of any of the persons hereinafter appointed respectively as persons before whom the execution of instruments executed beyond the limits of the said Province may be proved.

Proof of transmission by bankruptcy, marriage, will, or intestacy.

42. If such transmission has taken place by virtue of the bankruptcy or insolvency of any proprietor, the said declaration shall be accompanied by such evidence as may, for the time being, be receivable in courts of justice in the said Province as proof of the title of parties claiming under any bankruptcy or insolvency; and if such transmission has taken place by virtue of the marriage settlement of a female proprietor, the said declaration shall be accompanied by such marriage settlement, or by a copy thereof duly authenticated, and a copy of the register of such marriage, or other legal evidence of the celebration thereof, and shall declare the identity of the said female proprietor; and if such transmission has taken place by virtue of any will or testamentary instrument, then if such will or testamentary instrument shall have been made in the said Province, the said declaration shall be accompanied by such will; and if made in England, Wales, or Ireland, the said declaration shall be accompanied by such will, or by the probate thereof; and if made in Scotland, or in any British Possession, or in any foreign country, such declaration shall be accompanied by such will, or by any copy thereof, that may be evidence by the laws of Scotland, or of such possession or foreign country; and if such transmission shall have taken place in consequence of an intestacy, then, if such intestacy shall have occurred in the said Province, or in England, Wales, or Ireland, the said declaration shall be accompanied by the letters of administration or an official copy thereof; and if in Scotland, or in any British Possession, or foreign country, then by letters of administration, or any copy thereof, or by such other documents as by the laws of Scotland, or of such possession, or foreign country, may be receivable in the Courts of Judicature thereof as proof of intestacy, together with such documentary or other evidence as may be sufficient to prove the title of such declarant to the estate or interest in such land, according to the laws for the time being in force in the said Province.

43. The Registrar-General, upon the receipt of such declaration, so accompanied as aforesaid, shall, in the case of insolvency, or marriage settlement, enter the name of the person, entitled under such transmission, in the register book as owner of the estate or interest so transmitted, and shall file such declaration in his office, and shall also endorse on the grant or certificate of title of the land in which the estate or interest is transmitted, or as the case may be, on the bill of mortgage, bill of encumbrance, lease, or other instrument evidencing title to the estate or interest transmitted, a memorandum stating the day and hour on which such transmission had been recorded in the register book as aforesaid.

Registration of land transmitted by marriage or insolvency.

44. In the case of transmission by will, or in consequence of an intestacy, the Registrar-General, upon receipt of such declaration, so accompanied as aforesaid, shall give notice by advertisement, published once in each of two successive weeks in the *South Australian Government Gazette*, and in at least one newspaper published in the City of Adelaide, that he has received such declaration, which notice shall be in form of the Schedule hereto annexed, marked J, or in words to the like effect; and the Registrar-General shall cause copy of such notice to be posted in a conspicuous place in his office, and in such other public place as he may deem necessary; and in any such case, if the Registrar-General shall not, within the space of one calendar month from the date of the latest of such advertisements, receive any caveat forbidding compliance with such application, he shall enter the name of the person entitled under such transmission, in the register book, as owner of the estate or interest so transmitted; and shall, in other respects, proceed as hereinbefore directed for the case of a transmission by insolvency; and the Registrar-General, if he shall receive any such caveat within the time for such case above limited, shall, if the party lodging the same show reasonable grounds for so doing, suspend action in the matter, until such caveat shall have been withdrawn or until a decision shall have been obtained from the Court, having jurisdiction in the matter; and every person who shall fail to show reasonable cause for lodging such caveat to the satisfaction of the Judge, before whom any prosecution or suit may in such case be instituted, shall forfeit and pay a penalty not exceeding One Hundred Pounds.

Registration of transmission by will or intestacy.

Caveat may be lodged by parties interested.

Action to be suspended if caveat lodged.

45. No transmission of land under the operation of this Act either by descent, will, appointment of assignees or trustees, vesting order, letters of administration, order of the Supreme Court, or otherwise howsoever, by any

Transmission not valid against subsequent purchase unless registered.

proceeding filed of record, shall be valid and effectual against any subsequent purchaser, mortgagee, or lessee, unless legal evidence of heirship, the probate or exemplification of probate of such will, appointment of assignees or trustees, vesting order, letters of administration, order of the Supreme Court, or other instrument hereinbefore required to be in such case produced, has been so produced to the Registrar-General, and the particulars of the transmission entered in the register book.

Power of Court to prohibit transfer.

46. It shall be lawful for the Supreme Court, without prejudice to the exercise of any other power such Court may possess, upon the summary application of any person interested in transmitted land, made either by petition or otherwise, and either *ex parte,* or upon service of notice on any other person, as the Court may direct, to issue an order prohibiting for a time to be named in such order any dealing with such land; and it shall be in the discretion of such Court to make or refuse any such order, and to annex thereto any terms or conditions it may think fit, and to discharge such order when granted with or without costs, and generally to act in the premises in such manner as the justice of the case may require; and the Registrar-General, without being made a party to the proceedings, upon being served with such order or an official copy thereof, shall obey the same.

Land under operation of this Act, how leased.

47. When any land under the operation of this Act is intended to be leased or demised for a term of years, the proprietor shall execute a lease in form of the Schedule hereto annexed marked C, or as near thereto as circumstances permit, and every such lease shall contain the same description that is given in the grant or certificate of title or such other description as may be sufficient to identify the land intended to be leased, and shall be attested by a witness; and such lease when so executed, together with the grant, certificate of title, or other instrument evidencing the title of such proprietor to an estate in such land, shall be presented to the Registrar-General, who shall record in the register book the date and hour of such production to him, the date of the lease, the amount of rent or consideration money, the dates on which it is appointed to be paid, and the names and description of the proprietor and of the lessee, and shall record the like particulars by memorandum on the grant, certificate of title, or other instrument as aforesaid, and shall endorse on the lease a memorandum of the day and hour on which the said particulars had been entered in the register book, and shall authen-

Lease, if authenticated, to be evidence.

ticate such memorandum by signing his name and affixing his seal thereto; and every lease bearing such memorandum, so authenticated, shall be received as sufficient evidence of the title of the lessee to the estate or interest therein demised, and of all covenants, conditions, and restrictions therein expressly set forth, or by this Act declared to be implied against the lessor and lessee respectively.

48. A right to purchase land under the operation of this Act may be granted in any such lease by the words "that the said lessee shall have the option of purchasing the said land subject to such conditions, limitations, and restrictions as are herein specified;" which form of words shall operate as an expressed covenant in such lease, and shall apply as follows, that is to say— if the said lessee shall elect to purchase the said land, and shall in all respects comply with such conditions as may be expressed in such lease, or are by this Act declared to be implied therein, and shall pay the purchase-money therein mentioned, together with all rent, arrears of rent, and other moneys due and owing under or by virtue of such lease, then and in such case the lessor will execute a memorandum of sale of such land to such lessee, and will perform all acts and execute all instruments by this Act prescribed to be performed or executed by a vendor, in order to transfer to such lessee the estate or interest in such land specified.

49. The entry of every such lease in the register book, shall be held to transfer to the lessee an estate in such land as tenant, subject, nevertheless, to all such conditions and covenants as may be expressly set forth in such lease, if any, and to the conditions and covenants which are hereinafter declared to be implied against a lessor and against a lessee, or to all or any of such last-mentioned covenants as shall not be negatived or modified by express declaration in such lease or endorsed thereon: Provided always, that no lease of mortgaged land executed subsequent to the mortgage, shall be valid and binding against the mortgagee, unless such mortgagee shall have consented to such lease, in form and manner hereinafter provided.

50. Whenever any lease or demise for a term of years is intended to be surrendered, there shall be endorsed upon such lease the word "surrendered," with the date of such surrender, and upon such lease bearing such endorsement, signed by the lessee, and by the lessor accepting such surrender, and duly attested in manner hereinafter prescribed, being brought to the Registrar-General, he shall enter in the register book a memorandum recording the date of such surrender, and shall likewise endorse upon the lease a memorandum recording the fact of such entry having been made in the register book, and upon such entry being so made in the register book, the estate or interest of the lessee in such land shall revest in the lessor, or in such other person as, having regard to other intervening circumstances, if any, the same would be vested in had no such lease ever been executed, and the production of such lease bearing such endorsement authenticated by the hand and seal of the Registrar-General shall be sufficient evidence that such lease had been so surrendered.

Land may be pledged as security for a loan by bill of mortgage.

51. When any estate or interest in land, under the operation of this Act, is intended to be made security for a loan or other valuable consideration, the borrower shall execute a bill of mortgage, in form of the Schedule hereto annexed, marked D, or as near thereto as circumstances permit, and every such bill of mortgage shall contain an accurate statement of the estate or interest intended to be mortgaged, and such description as is given in the grant or certificate of title of the land in which such estate or interest is held, or such other description as may be necessary to identify such land, and shall be attested by a witness; and every bill of mortgage so executed, together with the grant or certificate of title of such land, or as the case may be, the lease or other instrument, proving the title of the mortgagor to such estate or interest in such land, shall be produced to the Registrar-General, who shall enter in the register book the date and hour of such production to him; the date of mortgage; the name, residence, and description of the mortgagor and of the mortgagee; the amount of consideration money; the rate of interest, and the date, if any, appointed for the redemption of such mortgage; and the dates on which interest is appointed to be paid; and shall record the like particulars by a memorandum endorsed upon such grant or certificate of title, lease, or other instrument of title, and shall also endorse upon such grant or certificate of title, lease, or other instrument, a memorandum stating the day and hour of the day in which the particulars of such mortgage had been recorded in the register book, and, upon such entry being made, as aforesaid, in the register book, the estate or interest in the land referred to, and described in such bill of mortgage, shall be held by such mortgagor, subject to and liable for the payment of the principal sum and interest therein set forth, at the times and under the conditions and covenants therein prescribed, or hereafter declared to be implied in bills of mortgage.

Payments by instalments, and extension of time.

52. The repayment of any sum of money by weekly instalments, or other periodical payments, may be secured on any land or on any estate or interest therein, by bill of mortgage, in the form or to the effect of the said Schedule D to this Act annexed, by varying such form so as to express fully the terms and modes and plan of payment of such sum of money: Provided also, that

the period of time hereinafter limited as the period after expiration of which it shall be lawful for a mortgagee to sell an estate pledged as security, in the event of default made in payment of interest or principal, or in the non-fulfilment of any covenant, may, by condition expressed in any such bill of mortgage, be extended or shortened, and, notwithstanding such variations in such form, the like covenants, rights, powers, and obligations, shall be implied thereunder and thereby, both against the mortgagor and the mortgagee as would be implied if no such variation had been made in the form of such Schedule.

53. In case default shall be made for the space of two calendar months in payment of the principal money or interest, or any part thereof, secured by any such bill of mortgage, so recorded as aforesaid, or if default shall be made in observance of any covenant that may be expressed in such bill of mortgage, or that is therein as against the mortgagor hereinafter declared to be implied, and the mortgagee shall have caused a written demand of payment of such principal sum or interest, or as the case may be, for the fulfilment of any such expressed or implied covenant, in respect to which such default may have been made, to be served on the mortgagor, or left at his last or usual place of abode, or if the mortgage be made by a corporate body, with the clerk thereof; and if default be made in either such respect for the further space of two calendar months from the service of such demand, then, in such case, it shall be lawful for the mortgagee to sell the estate or interest pledged to him as security by such bill of mortgage, or any part thereof, and either altogether or in lots, and either by public auction or private contract, or by both of such means, and subject to such conditions as he may think fit, and with power to buy in and resell the same, without being liable for any loss occasioned thereby, and to make and execute all such instruments, and to perform all such acts as in accordance with the provisions of this Act may be necessary for carrying into effect the powers hereby given, including the act of entering upon, and taking and giving possession to the purchaser of the land so pledged as security; all which sales, contracts, matters, and things hereby authorized, shall be as valid and effectual, as if the mortgagor had made, done, or executed the same; and the receipt or receipts in writing of the mortgagee shall be a sufficient discharge to any purchaser of any part of such mortgaged property, for so much of his purchase-money as may be thereby expressed to be received; no such purchaser shall be answerable for the loss, misapplication or nonapplication, or be obliged to see to the application of the purchase-money by him paid, nor shall he be concerned to inquire as to the fact of any such default or demand, as aforesaid, having

Mortgagee empowered to sell, if default be made in payment of interest, or principal, or in observance of covenants.

been made; the moneys to arise from such sale, as aforesaid, shall be applied: First—In payment of the expenses attending any such sale, or otherwise incurred in the execution of the power of sale hereby given: Secondly—In repayment of the principal money and interest remaining due, together with any costs and expenses occasioned by the non-payment thereof, or the non-observance of any such expressed or implied covenant; the surplus (if any) shall be paid to the mortgagor.

Estate or interest sold under bill of mortgage how passed.

54. The Registrar-General, in any such case as aforesaid, upon receipt of a memorandum of sale of such estate or interest, so pledged as aforesaid, signed by such mortgagee, together with proof to his satisfaction that all the requirements for such case by this Act provided have been duly executed and fulfilled, shall enter the particulars of such memorandum of sale in the register book, and record the fact of such entry by endorsement on such memorandum of sale, and shall in all other respects proceed in manner herein prescribed for the case of the transfer of a like estate or interest by the proprietor thereof, and every such transfer, when so recorded by the Registrar-General, shall be as valid and effectual to pass such estate or interest, as if the memorandum of sale had been executed by the mortgagor prior to the date of the execution of the bill of mortgage; and if such memorandum of sale shall purport to pass an estate in fee simple, and the existing grant or certificate of title be for that purpose surrendered to him, the Registrar-General shall make out and deliver to the purchaser a certificate of title to such land, having first endorsed thereon memoranda setting forth the particulars of all unsatisfied mortgages or other encumbrances, and of all leases, transfers, or other transactions affecting such land if any, which shall appear to have been registered and recorded upon such grant or certificate of title so surrendered, and shall in all other respects proceed as hereinbefore is directed in the case of the sale of an state in fee simple in land under the operation of this Act.

If an estate in fee simple.

Discharges of mortgage.

55. The Registrar-General, on the production of any bill of mortgage, executed under the provisions of this Act, and having thereon a receipt for the mortgage money duly signed and attested, shall make an entry in the register book to the effect that such mortgage has been discharged; and upon such entry being made, the estate, or interest, which by such bill of mortgage had been pledged as security for such loan, shall cease to be subject to or liable for the same, or any charges incident thereon, and the Registrar-General shall likewise endorse upon the grant or certificate of title, lease, or other instrument constituting or evidencing the title of the mortgagor to the

estate or interest in such land, a memorandum of the discharge of such mortgage, and of the date of such discharge, and shall cancel such bill of mortgage: Provided always, that if at or after the date appointed for the redemption of any such mortgage, the mortgagee shall be absent from this Colony, or shall not be in attendance to receive the mortgage money either personally, or by his attorney duly authorized in that respect, it shall be lawful for the Registrar-General to receive such mortgage money, with all arrears of interest then due thereon, in trust for such mortgagee, and the Registrar-General shall, thereupon, make entry in the register book discharging such mortgage, stating the day and hour in which such entry is made, and such entry shall be a discharge for such mortgage, valid to all intents, and shall have the same force and effect as is hereinbefore given to a like entry when made upon the production to the Registrar-General of the bill of mortgage, with the receipt of the mortgagee, and the Registrar-General shall, if demanded, give to the mortgagor a receipt for the money so paid to him in trust, and shall endorse on the grant, certificate of title, or other instrument, as aforesaid, and also on the bill of mortgage, whenever those instruments shall be brought to him for that purpose, the several particulars hereinbefore directed to be endorsed on each of such instruments respectively.

56. Whenever it is intended to render an estate or interest in land, under the operation of this Act, available for securing any dower, annuity, or sum of money, or to invest such estate or interest in trust, the proprietor shall execute a bill of encumbrance, in form of the Schedule hereto annexed marked E, or as near thereto as circumstances will permit; or, as the case may require, a bill of trust, in form of the Schedule hereto annexed marked F, or as near thereto as circumstances will permit, which bill of encumbrance or bill of trust shall be attested by a witness, and shall set forth the nature of the estate or interest intended to be encumbered or invested in trust; the amount of dower, or annuity, or sum of money for securing which such estate or interest is intended to be encumbered or invested in trust: the date on which, the manner in which, and the conditions or contingencies under which such dower, annuity, or sum of money is to become payable; and the uses, contingencies, restrictions, reversions, and remainders to which it is intended such dower, annuity, or sum of money should be subject or liable, if any, together with such description as may be sufficient to identify the land in which the estate or interest intended to be encumbered or vested in trust is held; and such bill of encumbrance, or bill of trust, together with the grant, certificate of title, lease, or other instrument, evidencing the title

*Land may be encumbered
for benefit of heirs,
or otherwise.*

of the encumbrancee to the estate or interest in such land intended to be encumbered or vested in trust shall be produced to the Registrar-General, who shall enter the particulars of such bill of encumbrance or bill of trust in the register book, and shall endorse upon the grant, certificate of title, lease, or other instrument, as aforesaid, a memorandum stating the date and hour of such production to him, for the purpose of such record being made, the date of the bill of encumbrance or bill of trust, the amount of the encumbrance, the contingencies, restrictions, reversions, and remainders, to which it is intended to be subject, if any, and the names and descriptions of the parties for whose benefit the same is created, or for whose uses such land is vested in trust, together with the names and descriptions of the trustees, if any, appointed, and upon such entry being made in the register book the estate or interest set forth in such bill of encumbrance or bill of trust shall become subject to and liable for the payment of such sums of money, dower, annuity, or other encumbrance in accordance with the conditions and limitations and subject to the covenants set forth in such bill of encumbrance or of trust, or which are hereinafter declared to be implied in any such instrument or as the case may be, such estate or interest shall become vested in the trustees named in such bill of trust, subject to such conditions and trusts as aforesaid.

Entry of discharge of encumbrance.

57. The Registrar-General, on the production of any bill of encumbrance, or of any bill of trust executed under the provisions of this Act, with a receipt for the amount of the encumbrance money, or trust money, endorsed thereon, duly signed and attested, or upon the receipt of proof to his satisfaction that the occurrence of the circumstances under which the amount of such encumbrance or trust could become chargeable against such land, in accordance with the conditions, limitations, and restrictions prescribed in such bill of encumbrance or bill of trust has ceased to be possible, shall make an entry in the register book to the effect that such encumbrance or trust has been discharged, or has lapsed, stating the day and hour in which such entry is made, and upon such entry being made, the interest, if any, which passed to the encumbrancee, or to the trustees under such bill of trust, shall vest in the same person or persons in whom the same would, having regard to intervening acts and circumstances, if any, have vested, if no such bill of encumbrance or bill of trust had ever been executed or made, and the Registrar-General shall thereupon cancel such bill of encumbrance or bill of trust, and shall also endorse on the grant, certificate of title, lease, or other instrument, constituting or evidencing the title of the encumbrancer to the estate or interest in the land referred to in such bill of encumbrance, a memorandum stating that such encumbrance had been discharged, and the date on which such entry of discharge had been made in the register book.

58. Every bill of mortgage, or bill of encumbrance, or of trust, shall be entered by the Registrar-General in the register book in the order of time in which the same is produced to him for that purpose; and the Registrar-General shall record by memorandum on such bill of mortgage, or bill of encumbrance, or of trust, that the same has been so entered by him, stating the day and hour of such entry, and shall certify such memorandum by signing the same and affixing his seal thereto, and every such bill of mortgage, bill of encumbrance, or of trust, so certified, shall be received in all Courts of Justice as sufficient evidence that the estate and interest therein described had been so mortgaged, encumbered, or vested in trust as the case may be, and of all other particulars therein contained.

Bills of mortgage, of encumbrance, and of trust to be recorded in order of time in which they are produced to Registrar-General, and endorsed.

35

59. If more than one mortgage, bill of encumbrance or of trust, be registered in respect to or affecting the same estate or interest in any land under the operation of this Act, the mortgagees, encumbrancees, and trustees, shall, notwithstanding any express, implied, or constructive notice, be entitled in priority one over the other according to the date at which each instrument is recorded in the register books, and not according to the date of each instrument itself.

Priority of mortgages.

60. When any estate or interest in land under the operation of this Act shall by bill of encumbrance, or bill of trust, be transferred to any person or body corporate, to the use of, or in trust for any other person, the whole legal ownership of such estate or interest shall vest in the person or body corporate to whom the same shall be so immediately and directly transferred; subject, however, to a trust for the benefit of such other person. Every limitation which before the passing of this Act might have been made by way of shifting, springing, or executory use, shall hereafter be made by transfer, in manner hereinbefore provided, without the intervention of uses, but not otherwise.

Legal estate shall vest in body corporate, or trustees under bill of trust.

61. No registered mortgage or encumbrance of any land under this Act shall be affected by any act of bankruptcy or insolvency committed by the mortgagor or encumbrancer, after the date of the entry in the register book of the bill of mortgage, bill of encumbrance, or bill of trust, creating such mortgage or encumbrance, notwithstanding such mortgagor, or encumbrancer, at the time of his becoming bankrupt may have in his possession and disposition

Rights of mortgagee or encumbrancee not affected by any act of bankruptcy of mortgagor.

and be the registered owner of such land; and such mortgage or encumbrance shall be preferred to any right, claim, or interest in such land, which may belong to the assignees of such bankrupt or insolvent.

36

Transfer of mortgage, and of encumbrance, and of lease.

62. A registered mortgage, a registered lease, or the interest of a registered encumbrancee of any land under this Act may be transferred to any person, by endorsement on the bill of mortgage, lease, bill of encumbrance, or bill of trust, which endorsement, shall be in the form of the Schedule hereto annexed marked O, or in words to the like effect; and on the production of such bill of mortgage, lease, or bill of encumbrance, so endorsed, to the Registrar-General, he shall enter in the register book the name of the transferree as mortgagee, lessee, or encumbrancee, of the land therein mentioned, and shall, by memorandum under his hand, record on such bill of mortgage, or bill of encumbrance, or lease, and, if the same be presented to him for that purpose, on the grant, certificate of title, or other instrument evidencing title to the estate or interest mortgaged or encumbered, that such transfer had been recorded by him, stating the date and hour of such record; and, upon such entry being so made, the estate or interest of the transferror, as set forth in such instrument, with all rights, powers, and privileges thereto belonging or appertaining, shall pass to the transferree; and such transferree shall thereupon become subject to and liable for all and every the same requirements and liabilities to which he would have been subject and liable if named in such instrument originally as mortgagee, encumbrancee, or lessee, of such land, estate, or interest, and the Registrar-General shall certify such endorsement by signing the same, and affixing his seal thereto, and every transfer, so certified, shall be received in evidence by any Court of Justice as sufficient evidence of its having been so entered in the register book.

General covenants to be implied in all instruments of transfer.

63. In every memorandum of sale, bill of mortgage, bill of encumbrance, bill of trust, lease, or other instrument of transfer, for valuable consideration, under provisions of this Act, there shall be implied the following covenants by each transferring party, severally for himself, to the extent of the interest departed with by him, that is to say—

(1.) That such transferring party hath good right and full power to transfer and assure the estate and interest purported to be transferred, and that free and clear from all encumbrances, other than such as are therein mentioned: That it shall be lawful for the party to whom such estate or interest is transferred quietly to enjoy the same, without any disturbance, by any act whatsoever, of such conveying party, or any person claiming under him, or by any rightful act of any other person:

(2.) That such transferring party will, at the cost of the party requiring the same, do all such acts and execute all such instruments as in accordance with the provisions of this Act may be necessary to give effect to all covenants, conditions, and purposes expressly set forth in such memorandum of sale, bill of mortgage, bill of encumbrance or trust, lease, or other instrument or transfer as aforesaid, or by this Act declared to be implied against the transferring party in any such instrument.

64. In every bill of mortgage, there shall be implied the following covenants against the mortgagor, that is to say—

Covenants to be implied in every bill of mortgage.

(1.) That he will pay the principal money, and interest thereby secured, after the rate, and at the times therein mentioned, without any deduction whatsoever:

(2.) That the mortgagor will repair and keep in repair all buildings or other improvements erected and made upon such land; and that the mortgagee may, at all convenient times, until such mortgage be redeemed, be at liberty, with or without surveyors or others, to enter into and upon such land, to view and inspect the state of repair of such buildings or improvements.

65. In every lease there shall be implied the following covenants against the lessee, that is to say—

Covenants to be implied in every lease against the lessee.

(1.) That he will pay the rent thereby reserved at the times therein mentioned, and all rates and taxes which may be payable in respect of the demised property, during the continuance of the lease:

(2.) That he will keep and yield up the demised property in good and tenantable repair:

66. In every lease there shall also be implied the following powers in the lessor, that is to say—

Powers to be implied in lessor.

(1.) That he may, by himself or his agents, at all reasonable times, enter upon the demised property, and view the state of repair thereof, and may serve upon the lessee, or leave at his last, or usual place of abode, a notice, in writing, of any defect, requiring him, within a reasonable time to be therein prescribed, to repair the same:

(2.) That whenever the rent reserved shall be in arrear for twenty-one days, he may levy the same by distress:

(3.) That in case the rent, or any part thereof, shall be in arrear for the space of six calendar months; or in case insurance as aforesaid shall not have been effected, or in case default in the fulfilment of any covenant expressly set forth in such lease as against the lessee shall not have been repaired, or in case the repairs required by such notice as aforesaid shall not have been completed within three calendar months after the service or leaving thereof, it shall be lawful for him to re-enter upon the demised property, and, upon proof of such re-entry, under any such circumstances, being made to the satisfaction of the Registrar-General, he shall note the same by entry in the register book, and the estate in the lessee in such land shall thereupon determine, but without releasing him from his liability in respect of the breach of any covenant in such lease expressed or implied.

Abbreviated forms of words for expressing covenants to be as effectual as if such covenants were set forth in words at length.

67. Such of the covenants hereinafter set forth as shall be expressed in any lease or mortgage, as to be implied against the lessee or mortgagor, shall, if expressed in the form of words hereinafter appointed and prescribed for the case of each covenant respectively, be so implied against such lessee or mortgagor as fully and effectually as if such covenants were set forth fully and in words at length in such lease or mortgage; that is to say, the words "that he will insure," shall imply as follows—that he will insure and so long as the term expressed in the said mortgage or lease shall not have expired, will keep insured, in some public insurance office, to be approved by such mortgagee or lessor, against loss or damage by fire, to the full amount specified in such lease or bill of mortgage, or if no amount be specified, then to their full value all buildings, tenements, or premises erected on such land, which shall be of a nature or kind capable of being insured against loss or damage by fire, and that he will, at the request of the mortgagee or lessor, hand over to, and deposit with him, the policy of every such insurance, and produce to him the receipt or receipts for the annual or other premiums payable on account thereof: Provided always, that all moneys to be received under or by virtue of any such insurance shall, in the event of loss or damage by fire, be laid out and expended in making good such loss or damage: Provided also, that if default shall be made in the observance or performance of the covenant last above-mentioned, it shall be lawful for the mortgagee or lessor, without prejudice nevertheless, to and concurrently with the powers granted him by his bill of mortgage or lease, in manner in and by this Act provided, to insure such building, and the costs and charges of such insurance shall, until such mortgage be redeemed, or such lease shall have expired, be a charge upon the said land; the words "and paint outside every

alternate year" shall apply as follows, viz.—and also will, in every alternate year, during the currency of such lease, paint all the outside woodwork and ironwork belonging to the hereditaments and premises mentioned in such lease, with two coats of proper oil-colors, in a workmanlike manner; the words "and paint and paper inside every third year" shall imply as follows, viz.—and will, in every third year, during the currency of such lease, paint the inside wood, iron, and other works now or usually painted with two coats of proper oil-color, in a workmanlike manner; and also repaper, with paper of a quality as at present, and such parts of the said premises as are now papered; and also wash, stop, whiten, or color such parts of the said premises as are now whitened or colored respectively; the words "and will fence" shall apply as follows, viz.—and also will, during the continuance of the said lease, erect and put up on the boundaries of the land therein mentioned, or upon such boundaries upon which no substantial fence now exists, a good and substantial fence capable of resisting the trespass of horses, oxen, bulls, and cows; the words "and cultivate" shall apply as follows, viz.—and will at all times during the said lease cultivate, use, and manage all such parts of the land therein mentioned as are or shall be broken up or converted into tillage in a proper and husbandlike manner, and will not impoverish or waste the same; the words "that the said lessee will not use the said premises as a shop" shall apply as follows, viz.—and also that the said lessee will not convert, use, or occupy the said hereditaments and premises mentioned in such lease, or any part thereof, into or as a shop, warehouse, or other place for carrying on any trade or business whatsoever, or permit or suffer the said hereditaments and premises, or any part thereof, to be used for any such purpose or otherwise than as a private dwelling-house, without the consent in writing of the said lessor; the words "and will not carry on offensive trades" shall apply as follows:—and also that no noxious, noisome, or offensive art, trade, business, occupation, or calling shall at any time during the said term be used, exercised, carried on, per-mitted, or suffered in or upon the said hereditaments and premises above mentioned, and that no act, matter, or thing whatsoever shall at any time during the said term be done in or upon the said hereditaments and premises, or any part thereof, which shall or may be or grow to the annoyance, nuisance, grievance, damage, or disturbance of the occupiers or owners of the adjoining lands and hereditaments; the words "and will not, without leave, assign, or sublet" shall apply as follows, viz.—and also that the said lessee shall not nor will during the term of such lease assign, transfer, demise, sublet, or set over, or otherwise by any act or deed procure the lands or premises therein mentioned, or any of them, or any part thereof, to be assigned, transferred, demised, sublet, or set over unto any person whomsoever without the consent in writing of the said lessor first had and obtained; the words "and will not cut timber" shall apply as follows—and also that the said lessee shall not nor will cut down, fell, injure, or destroy any growing or living timber, or timberlike trees, standing and being upon the said hereditaments and premises above mentioned, without the consent in writing of the said lessor; the words "and will carry on the business of a publican, and conduct the same in an orderly manner," shall apply as follows, viz.—and also that the said lessee will, at all times during the currency of such lease, use, exercise, and carry on, in, and upon the premises therein mentioned, the trade or business of a licensed victualler or publican and retailer of spirits, wines, ale, beer, and porter, and keep open and use the messuage, tenement, or inn, and buildings standing and being upon the said land as and for an inn or public-house for the reception, accommodation, and entertainment of travellers, guests, and other persons resorting thereto or frequenting the same, and manage and conduct such trade or business in a quiet and orderly manner, and will not do, commit, or permit, or suffer to be done or committed, any act, matter, or thing whatsoever, whereby or by means whereof any licence shall or may be forfeited or become void or liable to be taken away, suppressed, or suspended in any manner howsoever; the words "and will apply for renewal of licence" shall apply as follows, viz.— and also shall and will from time to time during the continuance of the said term, at the proper times for that purpose, apply for and endeavor to obtain, at his own expense, all such licences as are or may be necessary for carrying on the said trade or business of a licensed victualler or publican, in and upon the said hereditaments and premises, and keeping the said messuage, tenement, or inn open as and for an inn or public-house as aforesaid; the words "and will facilitate the transfer of licence" shall apply as follows, viz. and also shall and will, at the expiration or other sooner determination of the said lease, sign and give such notice or notices, and allow such notice or notices of a renewal or transfer of any licence as may be required by law to be affixed to the said messuage, tenement, or inn, to be thereto affixed, and remain so affixed during such time or times as shall be necessary or expedient in that behalf, and generally to do and perform all such further acts, matters, and things, as shall be necessary to enable the said lessor, or any other person authorized by him, to obtain the renewal of any licence, or any new licence, or the transfer of any licence then existing and in force.

Powers implied in every bill of encumbrance or

68. In every transfer of land under a bill of encumbrance, or of trust, by way of marriage settlement, there shall be implied the following powers in every tenant for life, in possession of the property or of any undivided share thereof, or in his guardian, or in the committee of his estate, or in case there shall be no tenant for life in possession, then in the trustees of the settlement, that is to say—that he or they may demise or lease, or concur in respect of such share in demising or leasing the property, estate or interest in settlement, for any term not exceeding twenty-one years, to take effect in possession at a reasonable yearly rent, without taking any fine or premium for the making such lease, and so that the lessee or lessees do execute a counterpart thereof.

trust by way of marriage settlement to be vested in tenant for life, his guardian, or in committee, or trustees of settlement.

69.   There shall also be implied in the trustees of the settlement, at the request in writing of any tenant for life in possession, or his guardian, or Committee; or if there be no such tenant for life, then at their own discretion, the following powers, that is to say—that they may dispose of the property in settlement, or any part thereof, either by way of sale, or in exchange for other property of the like nature and tenure, situated within the said Province; or where such property shall consist of an undivided share, may concur in the partition of the entirety of such property; and may give or take any money by way of equality of exchange or partition: Provided that the moneys to arise from any such sale, or be received for equality of exchange or partition, shall, with all convenient speed, be laid out in the purchase of other property, of like nature and tenure, situate within the said Province; and, moreover, any property so purchased or taken in exchange, shall be settled in the same manner and subject to the same trusts, powers, and provisoes, as the property so sold or given in exchange: Provided also, that until the moneys received in consequence of such sale, or exchange, or partition, shall be laid out as aforesaid, the same shall be invested on real security in the said Province, or in Government securities, and the interest thereof shall be paid to the persons entitled to the rents and profits of the property in settlement.

Powers implied in trustees of settlement.

They may dispose of or exchange property in settlement, or may agree to partition of undivided share.

Moneys realized by sale, or for equality of exchange, to be reinvested in real estate.

Moneys ad interim to be vested in real security, or Government securities.

70.   In every memorandum of sale or other instrument executed by a trustee, as trustee only, and not as the person beneficially interested in the land thereby contracted to be transferred or otherwise dealt with, there shall be implied a covenant only that such trustee hath not at any time before the execution of such memorandum of sale or other instrument done, or knowingly suffered to be done, any act, matter, or thing, whereby or by means whereof the land therein referred to can or may be impeached, charged, encumbered, or in any manner prejudicially affected in title, estate, or otherwise howsoever.

Covenants implied on the part of trustees.

Such covenants may be set forth in declaration, in actions for breach.

71. Where any memorandum of sale or other instrument in accordance with the provisions of this Act, is executed by more parties than one, such implied covenants shall be construed to be several and not to bind the parties jointly, and in any declaration in an action for a supposed breach of any such covenants, the covenant alleged to be broken may be set forth, and it shall be lawful to allege that the party against whom such action is brought did so covenant precisely in the same manner as if such covenant had been expressed in words in such memorandum of sale or other instrument, any law or practice to the contrary notwithstanding.

Construction of covenants binding heirs.

72. That when the deceased owner shall by any instrument or covenant bind or have bound his heirs, the term "heirs" shall be construed to mean the person or several persons who by law shall be chargeable with the debts of such deceased owner.

Covenants implied against a wife held to be implied against her husband.

73. In every case where any of the covenants or powers aforesaid would be implied by or in any woman if unmarried, the same shall be implied by or in her husband if she shall be married.

Covenants declared to be implied to have the same force as if the same had been expressed.

74. Every covenant which shall be implied by virtue of this Act shall have the same force and effect, and be enforced in the same manner as if it had been set out at length in the instrument wherein the same shall be implied.

Covenants declared to be implied may be negatived or modified.

75. Every covenant and power to be implied in any instrument by virtue of this Act may be negatived or modified by express declaration on the instrument, or endorsed thereon.

Vendor to have no equitable lien by reason of balance of purchase-money unpaid.

76. No vendor of any land under the operation of this Act shall have any equitable lien thereon by reason of the non-payment of the purchase-money, or any part of the purchase-money, for the same.

No contract for sale or dealing with land in futuro to be registered.

77. Except as hereinbefore provided in the case of right of purchase covenanted in a lease, no agreement for the sale, lease, or other dealing with any estate or interest in land under the operation of this Act to be performed *in futuro*, shall be entered in the register book; but any person claiming an interest in any such land under any such contract or agreement, or having any claim or interest adverse to any will may, by caveat in the form of the Schedule hereto marked P, or as near thereto as circumstances will permit, forbid the registration of any will or other instrument affecting such land, estate, or interest.

78. The proprietor of land under the operation of this Act, or any person registered as having estate or interest therein, may authorize and appoint any person to act for him, or on his behalf, in respect to the leasing of such land, or the sale or mortgage of his estate or interest therein, or otherwise lawfully to deal with such land, in accordance with the provisions of this Act, by executing a power in form of the Schedule hereto marked G, or as near thereto as circumstances will permit, which power shall contain the same description of such land as is contained in the grant, or existing certificate of title thereof, or such other description as may be sufficient to identify the said land, and shall set forth accurately the estate or interest of such proprietor in the said land, and shall specify the nature of the power intended to be conferred, the name and description of the person by whom, the places where, and the time within which it is to be exercised; and upon such power being brought to the Registrar-General, he shall enter the particulars of the same in the register book, and shall record upon such power a memorandum of the day and hour on which the said particulars were so entered, and shall authenticate such record by signing the same and affixing thereto his seal; and from and after the date of such entry in the register book, all acts lawfully done or performed by the person so appointed under authority of and within the limits prescribed in such power, shall have the same force and effect, and be equally binding on such proprietor, as if the said acts had been done or performed by such proprietor; and every such power bearing such endorsement, authenticated as aforesaid, shall be received in evidence as sufficient proof that the person to whom such power has been granted is duly authorized to make all contracts, to sign all instruments, and to perform all other lawful acts in accordance with the powers therein limited and appointed for the attainment of the objects therein specified, or any of them: Provided always, that nothing herein contained shall be interpreted to invalidate any power of attorney executed without the limits of the said Province, or prior to the passing of this Act, although such power may not be in accordance with the provisions of this Act.

Power of attorney.

43

Saving powers executed prior to this Act, or without the limits of the Province.

79. The Registrar-General, upon the application of any registered proprietors of land under the operation of this Act, shall grant to such proprietor a registration abstract enabling him to sell, mortgage, or otherwise deal with his estate or interest in such land at any place without the limits of the said Province, which registration abstract shall be in the form in the Schedule hereto marked H, or as near to such form as circumstances will permit, and the Registrar-General shall at the same time enter in the register book a memorandum recording the issue of such registration abstract, and shall

Registration abstract for registering dealings without the limits of the Province.

endorse on the grant, certificate of title, or other instrument evidencing or constituting the title of such applicant proprietor to such estate or interest a like memorandum recording the issue of such registration abstract, and from and after the issuing of any such registration abstract, no sale, mortgage, lease, or other transaction transferring, encumbering, or in any way affecting the estate or interest in respect of which such registration-abstract is issued shall be entered in the register book until such abstract shall have been surrendered to the Registrar-General to be cancelled, or the loss or destruction of such abstract proven to his satisfaction, or until the same shall have been revoked in manner hereinafter provided.

Mode of procedure under registration abstract.

80. Whenever any sale, mortgage, or lease is intended to be transacted under any of such registration abstract, a memorandum of sale, bill of mortgage, or lease as the case may require, shall be prepared in duplicate in the forms for such case hereinbefore appointed and prescribed, or as near to such form as circumstances will permit, and shall be produced to some one of the persons hereinafter appointed as persons before whom the execution of instruments without the limits of the said Province may be proven, and record shall be made upon such registration abstract of the several particulars hereinbefore required to be entered in the register book by the Registrar-General in the case of a transfer, mortgage, or lease, as the case may be, made within the limits of the said Province, and upon such record being authenticated by the signature of such authorized person as aforesaid, such transfer, mortgage, or lease shall be as valid and binding to all intents as if the same had been made within the limits of the said Province, and recorded in the register book by the Registrar-General, and subject to the rules hereinafter for each such case prescribed, every person whose name shall have been so recorded as purchaser, mortgagee, or lessee of such land upon such registration abstract, shall be held and taken to be registered as such, and shall have the same rights and powers, and be subject to the same liabilities as he would have had and been subject to if his name had been registered in the register book instead of on such abstract as proprietor, mortgagee, or lessee of such land or of such estate or interest therein.

General rules applicable to powers of attorney and registration abstracts.

81. The following rules shall be observed as to powers of attorney and registration abstracts:—

(1.) The power shall be exercised in conformity with the directions contained therein:

(2.) No sale, mortgage, or lease *bonâ fide* made thereunder shall be impeached by reason of the person by whom the power was given dying before the making of such sale, mortgage, or lease:

(3.) Whenever the power contains a specification of the place or places at which, and a limit of time within which, the sale is to be exercised, no sale, mortgage, or lease *bonâ fide* made to a purchaser, mortgagee, or lessee without notice shall be impeached by reason of the bankruptcy or insolvency of the person by whom the power was given:

(4.) If sale be effected, there shall be delivered up to the Registrar-General the memorandum of sale by which the land or any estate or interest therein is contracted to be transferred, the registration abstract, and the grant, certificate of title, lease, or other instrument of title; the Registrar-General shall enter in the register book a memorandum of the particulars of such sale, and of the cancelling of such abstract, and shall endorse on such memorandum, and also on the grant, certificate of title, lease, or other instrument of title a memorandum of the date and hour on which such entry was made, and if a full estate in fee simple, in such land, or in any part thereof, shall have been passed by such memorandum of sale, he shall cancel the grant or certificate of title delivered up, and shall issue a certificate of title of such land, or of the sold portion thereof to the purchaser, and if part only be sold, he shall also issue a certificate of title of the unsold portion to the proprietor; and shall, before issuing the same, endorse on each of such certificates of title, a memorandum of the particulars of all unsatisfied mortgages or encumbrances appearing in the registry book, or on the registration abstract affecting the land included under each such certificate of title respectively:

(5.) Every mortgage which is so endorsed as aforesaid on the registration abstract shall have priority over all bills of mortgages of the same estate executed subsequently to the date of the entry of the issuing of such abstract in the register book; and if there be more mortgages than one so endorsed, the respective mortgagees claiming thereunder shall, notwithstanding any express, implied, or constructive notice, be entitled one before the other according to the date at which a record of each instrument is endorsed on such abstract, and not according to the date of the bill of mortgage:

(6.) The discharge and also the transfer of any mortgage, so endorsed on such abstract may be endorsed on such abstract by any person hereinbefore authorized to record a mortgage thereon upon the production of such evidence and the execution of such instruments as are hereinbefore required to be executed and produced to the Registrar on the entry of the discharge or transfer of a mortgage in the register book; and such endorsement, so made on such abstract, shall have the same effect and be as valid, to all intents, as if such transfer or discharge had been entered in the register book by the Registrar-General in manner hereinbefore provided.

(7.) Upon proof, at any time, to the satisfaction of the Registrar-General that any power or registration abstract is lost, or so obliterated as to be useless, and that the powers thereby given have never been exercised, or if they have been exercised then upon proof of the several matters and things that have been done thereunder, it shall be lawful for the Registrar-General, with the sanction of the Lands Titles Commissioners, as circumstances may require, either to issue a new power or registration abstract, as the case may be, or to direct such entries to be made in the register book, or such other matter or thing to be done as might have been made or done if no such loss or obliteration had taken place.

(8.) Upon the delivery of any abstract to the Registrar-General, he shall, after recording in the register book in such manner as to preserve its priority, the particulars of every unsatisfied mortgage registered thereon, cancel such abstract, and enter the fact of such cancellation in the register book; and shall also, by endorsement on the grant, or certificate of title, lease, or other instrument, evidencing the title of such proprietor to such land, note the particulars of every such unsatisfied mortgage, and of every such lease, and the cancellation of such certificate of mortgage, and every certificate so cancelled shall be void to all intents, and shall file in his office the duplicates of every memorandum of sale, bill of mortgage, lease, or other instrument executed thereunder, which may for that purpose be delivered to him.

Revocation of power of attorney.

82. The registered owner for the time being of any land in respect of which a power of attorney has been issued may, by an instrument, under his hand, in the form Q in the Schedule hereto, or as near thereto as circumstances will permit, revoke such power; and if the holder of such power shall neglect or refuse to surrender the same to such owner, or his agent exhibiting such revocation order, duly certified by the Registrar-General, he shall be guilty of a misdemeanor, and on conviction thereof shall forfeit and pay a sum not exceeding One Hundred Pounds, unless it shall be made to appear to the satisfaction of the Court before whom the case may be tried, that the powers given therein had been exercised prior to the presentation of such revocation order.

83. After the presentation of such revocation order to the holder of such power, the said power shall, so far as concerns any mortgage or sale to be thereafter made, be deemed to be revoked and of no effect.

Power of attorney rendered null by revocation order.

84. Whenever it is intended that partition should be made by copartners, joint tenants, or tenants in common, of any land under the operation of this Act, or of any estate or interest in such land, such copartners, joint tenants, or tenants in common, may execute a memorandum of sale, lease, or other such instrument of transfer as in accordance with the provisions of this Act the nature of the estate or interest may require, purporting to sell, lease, or otherwise transfer, to each or any of such copartners, joint tenants, or tenants in common respectively, such part of the said land, or their estate or interest in such part of the said land as shall be expressed and described in such memorandum of sale, lease, or instrument of transfer; and upon such memorandum of sale, lease, or other instrument being presented to the Registrar-General, he shall enter the particulars of the same in the register book, and proceed in other respects as is hereinbefore directed for the case of the transfer of a like estate or interest in land under the operation of this Act, and upon such entry being made in the register book, the estate or interest of such copartners, joint tenants, or tenants in common, in the particular piece of land described in such memorandum of sale, lease, or other instrument, shall pass from such copartners, joint tenants, or tenants in common, and shall vest in the individual named and described as purchaser, lessee, or transferee, of the estate or interest of such copartners, joint tenants, or tenants in common, as set forth, limited, and described in such memorandum of sale, lease, or other instrument of transfer.

Partition of copartnerships, or joint tenancy, or tenancy in common.

47

85. If the consent or direction of any person shall be requisite or necessary upon a sale or other disposition of land under the operation of this Act, or any estate or interest therein, such consent or direction may be endorsed upon the memorandum of sale, or other instrument executed for the purpose of transferring, or otherwise dealing with such land, or estate or interest therein, in the words following, that is to say—"I consent hereto," which consent or direction, when signed by such consenting or directing party, and attested in manner hereinafter prescribed, shall have full validity and effect.

Consent may be given by endorsement.

86. Every instrument signed by any married woman, as a vendor, mortgagor, or lessor, or otherwise, for the purpose of disposing of, releasing, surrendering, or extinguishing any estate, right, title, or interest in any land under the operation of this Act, if produced and acknowledged by her in manner provided by the Ordinance of the Governor in Council of the said

Validity given to acts of married women.

Province, No. 15 of 1845, intituled "An Ordinance to render effectual Conveyances by Married Women, and to declare the effect of certain Deeds relating to Dower," shall have the same effect and validity as is by this given to instruments of the like nature when signed by male persons of full age and sound mind, attested in manner hereinbefore prescribed.

Provision for cases of infancy or other incapacity.

87. If any person interested in any land under the operation of this Act is, by reason of infancy, lunacy, or other inability, incapable of making any declaration or doing anything required or permitted by this Act to be made or done by a proprietor in respect of registry, transfer, or transmission, mortgage, or encumbrance of such land, or the release of the same from any mortgage or encumbrance, or the leasing, assigning, or in any other manner dealing with such land, then the guardian or committee, if any, of such incapable person, or, if there be none, any person appointed by any Court or Judge possessing jurisdiction in respect of the property of incapable persons, upon the petition of any person on behalf of such incapable person, or of any other person interested in the making such declaration, or doing such thing, may make such declaration, or a declaration as nearly corresponding thereto as circumstances permit, and do such thing in the name and on behalf of such incapable person; and all acts done by such substitute shall be as effectual as if done by the person for whom he is substituted.

Execution of instruments, before whom to be proved.

88. The execution of any instrument made in accordance with the provisions of this Act, or the discharge of any mortgage or encumbrance, or the transfer or surrender of any lease, may be proved, if the parties executing the same be resident within ten miles of the Registry Office, then before the Registrar-General; if the parties executing the same be resident at a distance from the Registry Office greater than ten miles, then before the Registrar-General or a Justice of the Peace; if the said parties be resident in Great Britain, then by the Mayor or other Chief Officer of any Corporation, or before a Notary Public; if the said parties be resident in any British Possession, then before the Chief Justice, Judge of any Superior Court having jurisdiction in such Possession, or before the Governor, Government Resident, or Chief Secretary thereof; if the said parties be resident at any foreign place, then before the British Consular Officer resident at such place; and a certificate of such proof, under the hand and seal of the Registrar-General, or of any such Justice of the Peace, Notary Public, Mayor, or other Chief Officer, Chief Justice, Judge, Governor, Resident, Chief Secretary, or Consular Officer, as the case may be, shall be sufficient evidence that the execution of such instrument, had been duly proved.

89. The execution of any such instrument, release, transfer, or surrender, may be proved before any such person as aforesaid, by the oath or solemn affirmation of the parties executing the same, or of a witness attesting the signing thereof; and if such witness shall answer in the affirmative, each of the questions following, that is to say—

Are you the witness who attested the signing of this instrument, and is the name or mark purporting to be your name or mark as such attesting witness your own handwriting?

Do you personally know   , the person signing this instrument, and whose signature you attested?

Is the name purporting to be his signature his own handwriting—is he of sound mind—and did he freely and voluntarily sign the same?

Then the Registrar-General, Justice, or other person before whom such witness shall prove such signature as aforesaid, shall endorse upon such instrument a certificate in form of the Schedule hereto annexed marked R, or as near thereto as circumstances will permit: Provided also, that, if any person signing any such instrument, transfer, release, or surrender, as aforesaid, as the maker thereof, shall be personally known to the Registrar-General, Justice, or other person as aforesaid, it shall be lawful for such person to attend and appear before such Registrar-General, Justice, or other person to whom he is personally known, and then and there acknowledge that he did freely and voluntarily sign such instrument, transfer, release, or surrender; and upon such acknowledgment, the Registrar-General, Justice, or other person, as the case may be, shall endorse on such instrument a certificate, in the form or to the effect of the Schedule hereto marked S, or as near thereto as circumstances will permit, and it shall not be necessary for such instrument to be proved by the attesting witness in manner aforesaid: Provided also that such questions as aforesaid may be varied as circumstances shall or may require, in case any person shall sign such instrument by his mark: Provided also, that, on the signing of any such instrument by any married woman, and the acknowledgment thereof by her in manner mentioned or referred to in this Act, no further or other proof or acknowledgment shall be requisite or necessary.

Mode of proving instruments.

90. Every such Justice as aforesaid, sitting in open Court, shall be, and he is hereby required to administer the oath, or take the solemn affirmation, or the acknowledgment, of any person attending before him for the purpose of proving or acknowledging any such instrument as aforesaid.

Justices required to administer oath.

91. It shall not be lawful for any person to institute or prosecute any action of ejectment for the recovery of land under the operation of this Act, against

No action of ejectment to be instituted against

person registered as proprietor.

the registered proprietor, save and except only in the case of a mortgagee against his mortgagor, an encumbrancee against his encumbrancer, or a lessor against his lessee, in default, under the terms, conditions, or covenants of a bill of mortgage, bill of encumbrance, bill of trust, or lease, as the case may be, executed and registered in accordance with the provisions of this Act, or in the case of any person duly authorized by any Court having jurisdiction in cases of bankruptcy or insolvency, against a bankrupt or insolvent, or in case the registered proprietor has obtained such land by fraud or misrepresentation.

Compensation in case of error or fraud.

92. Any person who shall, by the decree of any Court having jurisdiction in such case, be declared to be the lawful heir to any land under the operation of this Act, or any person who shall by any such decree be declared to have been deprived of an estate or interest in such land, through the entry in the register book of any memorandum of sale or other instrument affecting such land, made, or procured to be made by fraud, error, misrepresentation, oversight, or deceit, may bring and prosecute an action at law in the Supreme Court for the recovery of damages against the person who may, by fraud or other means as aforesaid, have become registered as proprietor of such land; and the Court or Jury before whom such action is tried shall, if such person obtains a verdict in his favor, find damages against the person so registered as proprietor through fraud, or error, or other means aforesaid, for such sum of money as the Court or Jury may think fit, not exceeding the value of such land at the time when such person did so wrongfully, or in error become registered as proprietor of the same, together with interest on the amount of such value, computed at Six Pounds in the One Hundred Pounds per annum, from the date when such person so became wrongfully, or in error, registered as proprietor.

Person registered in error may retransfer land, in lieu of paying damages.

93. In case the person against whom damages shall in any such case be awarded, shall have been so registered as proprietor, through error or misconception, and not through fraud, misrepresentation, or deception, it shall be lawful for such last-named person, in lieu of paying such sums of money so awarded as damages (if he shall so elect and is in a position so to do), to transfer such land to the person who shall have obtained such verdict, clear of any mortgage, encumbrance, or any lien or liability of such nature or amount as to reduce the value of the said land, estate, or interest below the amount so awarded as damages; and the memorandum of sale, or other instrument evidencing transfer of such land, estate, or interest to the person who shall have obtained such verdict, duly executed and registered in accordance with the provisions of this Act, shall be received in any Court of Law or Equity as a sufficient discharge for the liability on account of the sum of money so awarded as damages.

94. If it shall be made to appear, to the satisfaction of the Court before whom such action shall be tried, that any person, at the time then being registered as proprietor in respect of such estate or interest, has been so registered through fraud or misrepresentation, or in any manner otherwise than as purchaser, or mortgagee for *bona fide* valuable consideration, or by transfer, or transmission from or through a purchaser or mortgagee for *bona fide* valuable consideration, it shall be lawful for such Court to direct the Registrar-General to cancel the entry in the register book recording the proprietorship of the person who shall by such fraud or misrepresentation have been so registered, together with all subsequent entries therein relating to the same estate or interest, and the Registrar-General shall obey such order; and the estate or interest referred to in such order shall thereupon revert to and vest in the persons in whom (having regard to intervening circumstances, if any) the same would have vested had no such entries been so made in the register book.

95. If, at the date of making such decree as aforesaid, the person who shall, by fraud, misrepresentation, or error, have been registered as proprietor of the estate or interest therein referred to, shall still be registered as proprietor of the same estate, or of any portion thereof, notice of such decree, signed by the Master of the Supreme Court, or by the Judge by whom such decree was made, served upon the Registrar-General, shall operate as a destringas, and the Registrar-General, upon the receipt of such notice, and until the damages awarded shall be paid or satisfied, shall abstain from recording on the register book any transfer, mortgage, or other transaction, affecting the same estate or interest, except for the purpose of satisfying such award in manner hereinbefore provided.

96. In case the person against whom such verdict shall have been obtained shall fail to pay, within reasonable time, the amount of damages so awarded, or to convey the estate or interest to the person who shall have obtained such verdict, the amount of such award may be levied by distress upon the goods of such person, or he may be attached, and lodged in the common gaol in Adelaide until such amount be paid or satisfied in manner aforesaid: and, in case of a return of *nulla bona*, or if the amount recovered by such distress shall not suffice to cover the amount of damages so awarded, to-

gether with all costs of suit, the Registrar-General shall address to the Treasurer of the said Province, a requisition for the payment of the amount so awarded, or of the balance thereof, and the said Treasurer upon receipt of such requisition, and of a warrant under the hand of the Governor, countersigned by the Chief Secretary of the said Province, shall pay such amount, and shall charge the same to the account of the assurance fund hereinbefore described.

Failing recovery, amount to be made good out of assurance fund.

Period within which actions may be brought.

97. No action of ejectment, or for recovery of damages, shall be in any case instituted against any registered proprietor after the expiration of the time within which it shall be lawful, by any law for the time being in force in the said Province, to bring or commence an action for ejectment for the recovery of any land.

Recovery of certificate issued in error, or in consequence of fraudulent representation.

98. If any certificate of title, or other instrument affecting land, under the operation of this Act, or any entry, memorandum, or endorsement, in or upon any such instrument, shall be obtained from or issued by the Registrar-General through or by means of fraud, error, misrepresentation, oversight, or deceit, it shall be lawful for the said Registrar-General, by summons under the hand of a Judge of the Supreme Court, to be issued to such Registrar-General upon verbal application made by him, to summon the person to whom such certificate, or other instrument, shall have been issued, to surrender and yield up such certificate, or other instrument, to such Registrar-General; and if such person shall neglect or refuse to surrender and yield up such certificate, or other instrument, it shall be lawful for the said Court, or any Judge thereof, upon proof that such summons had been duly served, and upon the like application of the Registrar-General, to issue an attachment against such person, and commit him to the common gaol at Adelaide, until such certificate, or other instrument, be surrendered and yielded up; and the Registrar-General shall give public notice, by advertisement, published once in each of three successive weeks in the *South Australian Government Gazette*, and at least one newspaper published in the City of Adelaide, that such certificate, or other instrument, or such entry, memorandum, or endorsement, had been obtained or issued in manner as aforesaid, and shall declare such certificate, or other instrument, or such entry, memorandum, or endorsement, to be void, and of no effect whatever; whereupon the same shall become void and of no effect: Provided always, that nothing herein contained shall be held to operate in any such manner as to subject to impeachment or to defeat the title of any person who, before the issue of such summons as aforesaid, shall, upon payment of *bona fide* valuable consideration, have become registered as proprietor in respect to the estate or interest referred to in such certificate, entry, memorandum, or endorsement.

99. In the event of the grant or certificate of title of any land registered under this Act being lost, mislaid, or destroyed, the proprietor of such land, together with other persons, if any, having knowledge of the circumstances, may make a declaration before the Registrar-General, stating the facts of the case, the names and descriptions of the registered owners, and the particulars of all mortgages, encumbrances, or other matters affecting such land and the title thereto, to the best of declarant's knowledge and belief; and the Registrar-General, if satisfied as to the truth of such declaration, and the *bonâ fides* of the transaction, may, with the consent of the Lands Titles Commissioners, issue to such applicant a provisional certificate of title of such land, which provisional certificate shall contain an exact copy of the original grant, or certificate of title, bound up in the register book, and of every memorandum and endorsement thereon at the time appearing, and shall also contain a statement of the circumstances under which such provisional certificate is issued; and the Registrar-General shall, at the same time, enter in the register book notice of the issuing of such provisional certificate, and the date thereof, and the circumstances under which it was issued; and such provisional certificate shall be available for all purposes and uses for which the grant, or certificate of title, so lost or mislaid would have been available, and as valid to all intents as such lost grant or certificate.

Provision in case of lost grant.

53

100. The Registrar-General, upon receipt of any caveat in accordance with the provisions of this Act, shall cause the same to be published in the *Government Gazette* of the said Province, and also in at least one newspaper published in the City of Adelaide, three several times in each of three successive weeks, at the expense of the person serving such caveat, and in case such person shall refuse to pay the expense thereof, the Registrar-General shall not be bound or obliged to receive such caveat.

Receipt of caveat to be published.

101. The Registrar-General shall give notice of the receipt of such caveat to every person registered as proprietor in respect to the estate or interest referred to in such caveat, and to every person presenting for purpose of registration any instrument relating to such estate or interest, and such registered proprietor, or other person claiming estate or interest in the same land, may, if he thinks fit, summon the person signing such caveat to attend before the Judges of the Supreme Court of the said Province, or one of them,

Notice of caveat to parties.

Person lodging caveat may be summoned to show cause.

to show cause why such caveat should not be withdrawn; and it shall be lawful for the said Court, or a Judge thereof, upon proof that such last-mentioned person has been summoned, to make such order in the premises, either *ex parte* or otherwise, as to the said Court or Judge shall seem fit.

Person entering caveat to establish his claim. Proceedings to be had thereon.

102. Within three calendar months from the entering of such caveat, the person entering the same shall take proceedings to establish his claim, and such proceedings shall be by way of petition to the Supreme Court, which shall be filed on oath, and shall contain, as concisely as may be, a statement of the material facts on which the petitioner relies, such statement to be divided into paragraphs, numbered consecutively, and each paragraph shall contain, as nearly as may be, a separate and distinct allegation, and shall state specifically what estate, lien, or charge the petitioner claims, and the said Court, upon receipt of such petition, shall issue an order appointing a time for hearing the same.

Copy of petition to be served upon claimant.

103. The petitioner shall cause a copy of such petition and of the order for hearing to be served upon the registered proprietor of the estate or interest in respect to which such caveat is lodged, or upon the person applying to have land brought under the operation of this Act as the case may be, fourteen days at least before the day appointed for the hearing of the said petition.

Showing cause on petition.

104. On the day of hearing, the claimant is personally, or by counsel, to show cause in Court if he can, and if necessary by affidavit, why the matters claimed by such petitioner should not be ordered.

Hearing of petition on non-attendance of claimant.

105. If the claimant shall not appear on the day appointed for the hearing, the Court may, upon due proof of the service of such petition and order, make such order, in the absence of the claimant, either for the establishment of the rights of the petitioner, or as the nature and circumstances of the case may require, as to such Court may seem meet.

Hearing of petition.

106. On the day appointed for the hearing of the petition, and on hearing the same, and the affidavits, if any, filed in support thereof, and hearing what may be alleged on behalf of the claimant, the Court may, if it shall think fit, make an order establishing the right of the petitioner, or directing any inquiries to be made, or other proceedings taken, for the purpose of ascertaining the rights of the parties, or may dismiss the petition.

107. The Supreme Court may, if it shall think fit, direct any question of fact brought before it to be decided before a Judge thereof; and for that purpose may direct an issue to be tried, wherein the petitioner shall be plaintiff, and the claimant shall be defendant; and the said Court shall direct when and where the trial of such issue shall take place, and shall also require the claimant and petitioner severally to name an attorney to act on his behalf; and the Court may also direct the parties to produce all deeds, books, papers, and writings, in their custody or power, on a day to be named by the Court, and each party shall have liberty to inspect the same, and take copies thereof, at their own expense; and such of them as either party shall give notice to have produced at the trial, shall be produced accordingly; and, in case the parties differ upon the question or questions to be tried, the Court may either settle the same, or otherwise refer it to the Lands Titles Commissioners.

Question of fact may be referred to a jury.

Parties to produce deeds, &c.

Form of issue.

108. If the Court shall find that the petitioner is entitled to all or some of the matters claimed by him, the order of the Court shall declare what is the estate, interest, lien, or claim to which the petitioner is entitled, and shall direct such order to be served upon the Registrar-General, who shall obey the same or act in accordance therewith.

Proceedings where petitioner establishes his claim.

109. Every order of the Court shall have such and the like effect as a decree or decretal order of the Court made in a suit commenced by bill, and duly prosecuted to a hearing, according to the present practice of the Equitable Jurisdiction of the Court.

Effect of order.

110. If, at the hearing of such petition, it shall appear to the Court that, for the purposes of justice, it is necessary or expedient that a bill should be filed, the Court may order or authorize such bill to be filed subject to such terms as to costs or otherwise as may be thought proper.

Court may require bill to be filed.

111. The Court shall have power in all cases to order the payment of the costs occasioned by entering the caveat or incidental thereto, to be paid by or to the petitioner, as the case may require and as the Court may think fit.

As to costs.

112. The procedure and practice in the matter of a petition presented under this Act shall, unless otherwise provided, be regulated by the procedure and practice of the Equitable Jurisdiction of the said Supreme Court in a claim filed under an Act passed in the year of our Lord one thousand eight hundred and fifty-three, and being numbered 14 of that year, intituled "An Act to amend the practice and proceeding in the Equitable Jurisdiction of the Supreme Court of South Australia."

Procedure to be regulated by Act No. 14, 1853.

Duplicates of future public maps to be deposited.

113. From and after the passing of this Act all public maps delineating the Waste Lands of the Crown in the said Province for the purpose of sale, shall be made in duplicate, and the Surveyor-General shall sign each duplicate, and shall certify the accuracy of the same, and such duplicates of such maps shall be deposited in the Registry Office, and whenever, in any instrument relating to land brought under the operation of this Act, and executed subsequent to the passing thereof, reference is made to the public maps of the said Province deposited in the office of the Surveyor-General, such reference shall be interpreted and taken to apply equally, and with the same force and effect, and for the same purposes, to either of such duplicates.

Proprietor may deposit map.

114. It shall be lawful for any proprietor, subdividing any land under the operation of this Act, for the purpose of selling the same in allotments as a township, to deposit with the Registrar-General a map of such township, provided that such map shall be on a scale of not less than one inch to the chain, and shall exhibit, distinctly delineated, all roads, streets, passages, thoroughfares, squares, or reserves, appropriated or set apart for public use, and also all allotments into which the said land may be divided, marked with distinct numbers or symbols, and the person depositing such map shall sign the same, and shall certify the accuracy thereof by declaration before the Registrar-General, or a Justice of the Peace.

Registrar-General may require map to be deposited.

115. It shall be lawful for the Registrar-General, if he shall think fit, to require the proprietor applying to have any land brought under the operation of this Act, or desiring to transfer or lease the same, or any portion thereof, to deposit, at the Registry Office, a map or plan of such land, and if the said land, or the portion thereof proposed to be transferred or leased, shall be of less area than one statute acre, then such map or plan shall be on a scale not less than one inch to the chain; and if such land, or the portion thereof, about to be sold or leased, shall be of greater area than one statute acre, then such map or plan shall be upon a scale not less than one inch to six chains, and such proprietor shall sign such map and shall declare to the accuracy of the same before the Registrar-General, or a Justice of the Peace; and if such proprietor shall neglect or refuse to comply with such requirement, it shall not be incumbent on the Registrar-General to proceed with the bringing of such land under the operation of this Act, or with the registration of such transfer or lease: Provided always, that subsequent subdivisions of the same land may be delineated on the map or plan of the same, so deposited, if such map be upon a sufficient scale, in accordance with the provisions herein contained, and such proprietor shall certify the correctness of the delineation of each such subdivision, by declaration in manner prescribed for the case of the deposit of an original map.

116. Any person may, upon payment of a fee specified in Schedule T hereto, have access to the register book for the purpose of inspection at any reasonable time during the hours and upon the days appointed for search.

Search allowed.

117. The Registrar-General, upon payment of such reasonable sum as may be appointed by any regulation made by him for such case, with sanction of the Governor, shall furnish to any person applying at a reasonable time for the same, a certified copy of any instrument affecting or relating to land registered under the provisions of this Act, and every such certified copy signed by him and sealed with his seal, shall be received in evidence in any Court of Justice, or before any person having by law, or by consent of parties, authority to receive evidence as *prima facie* proof of all the matters contained or recited in or endorsed on the original instrument, and the production of any such certified copy, so signed and sealed, shall be as effectual in evidence to all intents as the production of the original.

Certified copies signed and sealed to be furnished by Registrar-General and to be received in evidence.

118. The Registrar-General shall not be liable to damages or otherwise for any loss accruing to any person by reason of any act done or default made by him in his character of Registrar-General, unless the same has happened through his neglect or wilful act.

Indemnity to Registrar.

119. The Registrar-General shall keep a correct account of all such sums of money as shall be received by him in accordance with the provisions of this Act, and shall pay the same into the Public Treasury of the said Province at such times, and shall render accounts of the same to such persons, and in such manner as may be directed in any regulations that may for that purpose be prescribed by the Governor-in-Chief of the said Province, by and with the advice of the Executive Council thereof; and the Registrar-General shall address to the said Treasurer requisitions to pay moneys received by him, in trust or otherwise, on account of absent mortgagees or other persons entitled in accordance with the provisions of this Act; which requisitions, when proved and audited in manner directed, by any such regulations framed as aforesaid at the time being in force in the said Province, and accompanied by warrant for payment of the same under the hand of the Governor, countersigned by the Chief Secretary thereof, the said Treasurer shall be bound to obey, and all fines and fees received under the provisions of this Act, except fees payable to the Lands Titles Commissioners for the

Registrar-General to pay moneys into Treasury, and to render accounts.

Parties entitled to be paid by Treasurer, upon warrant signed by Registrar-General.

bringing of land under the operation of this Act, shall be carried to account by the said Treasurer as General Revenue.

Penalty for falsifying register book, or procuring entries or instruments by fraud or misrepresentation.

58

120. Any person who shall wilfully or knowingly, by fraud or misrepresentation, make, or cause, or obtain to be made in the register book, any entry which might in any way affect the right, title, estate, or interest of himself, or of any other person, in any land under the operation of this Act, or who shall wilfully or knowingly, by fraud or misrepresentation, procure from the Registrar-General any certificate of title, registration abstract, or other instrument evidencing or relating to title to, or estate or interest in land under the operation of this Act, or shall cause or procure to be made any entry, certificate, memorandum, or endorsement by this Act prescribed to be made in or upon any such certificate, abstract, or other instrument by the Registrar-General, or other authorized person, or who shall use or utter any such certificate, abstract, or other instrument, knowing the same to be counterfeited, forged, or altered, or to have been obtained by fraud or misrepresentation, or to contain or bear any entry, memorandum, certificate, or endorsement as aforesaid, forged, counterfeited, or altered, or obtained by fraud or misrepresentation, and who shall be thereof lawfully convicted, shall be deemed guilty of felony, and be sentenced to be imprisoned for any period not exceeding four years, and to be kept to hard labor or solitary confinement for any part of the period aforesaid; and if any person shall wilfully or knowingly make a false oath or affirmation touching or concerning any matter or procedure made or done in pursuance of this Act, and be thereof lawfully convicted, such person shall be deemed guilty of perjury, and be imprisoned for the period, and in the manner aforesaid, and, in addition to such punishment, any person damnified or suffering loss by any such fraud, misrepresentation, forgery, counterfeit, alteration, use, or utterance, of any such certificate, abstract, or other instrument, as aforesaid, or by the making of any such false oath or affirmation, shall have a right of action against, and be entitled to recover damages from, the person guilty of such fraud, misrepresentation, forgery, counterfeit, alteration, use, or utterance, or making such false oath or affirmation, the amount of all damages he may have sustained thereby, with full costs of suit, as hereinbefore provided.

Person making false oath or affirmation guilty of perjury, and liable to be imprisoned, in addition to damages recoverable by the party damnified.

Jurisdiction.

121. Unless in any case herein otherwise expressly provided, all offences against the provisions of this Act may be prosecuted, and all penalties or sums of money imposed or declared to be due or owing by or under the provisions of the same, may be sued for and recovered in the name of the Attorney-General, or of the Registrar-General, before any Court in the said

Province, having jurisdiction for punishment of offences of the like nature, or for the recovery of penalties or sums of money of the like amount.

122. It shall be lawful for the Registrar to charge and receive such fees as shall be appointed by the Governor of the said Province, by and with the consent of the Executive Council, not in any case exceeding the several fees specified in the Schedule hereto marked T.

Fees.

123. This Act shall commence and take effect from and after the first day of July, one thousand eight hundred and fifty-eight.

Commencement of Act.

SCHEDULES REFERRED TO.

A   SOUTH   *[Royal Arms.]*   AUSTRALIA.

Certificate of Title.

A. B., of *(here insert description, and if certificate be issued pursuant to any sale, reference to memorandum of sale, reciting particulars)* is now seised of an estate *(here state whether in fee simple)* subject nevertheless to such encumbrances, liens, and interests, as are notified by memorandum endorsed hereon, in that piece of land situated in the *(County, Hundred, or Township)* of   bounded on the *(here set forth boundaries, in chains, links, or feet)*, containing *(here state area)*, be the same a little more or less *(exclusive of roads intersecting the same, if any)*, with right of way over *(state rights of way, and other privileges, or easements, if any)*; plan of which piece of land is delineated in *(margin, or in map No   , deposited in Registry Office)*, which said piece of land is *(or is part of)* the *(Country Section, or Town allotment)*, marked   , delineated in the public map of the said *(County, Hundred, or Township)*, deposited in the office of the Surveyor-General, which was originally granted the   day of   , under the hand and seal of   Governor *(or Resident Commissioner)* of the said Province, to *C. D.*, of *(here insert description)*, as appears by *(land grant, former certificate, or other instrument of title, describing them)*, now delivered up and cancelled.

In witness whereof, I have hereunto signed my name, and affixed my seal, this   day of   .

Registrar-General   *(L. S.)*.

Signed, sealed, and delivered, in presence }
    of   the   day of }

B   SOUTH AUSTRALIA.

Memorandum of Sale.

I, *A. B.*, being seised of an estate *(here state nature of the estate or interest, whether in fee simple or life estate, or of a greater or less description than a life estate)*, subject, however, to such encumbrances, liens, and interests, as are notified by memorandum endorsed hereon, in that piece of land situated in the *(County, Hundred, or Township)* of   , bounded on the *(here set forth boundaries, in chains, links, or feet)*, containing *(here state area)*, be the same a little more or less *(exclusive of roads intersecting the same, if any)*, with right of way over *(here state rights of way, privileges, or easements intended to be conveyed)*; plan of which piece of land is delineated in *(margin, or in map No.   , deposited in the Registry Office)*, which said piece of land is *(or is part of)* the *(Country Section, or Town allotment)*, marked   , delineated in the public map of the said *(County, Hundred, or Township)*, deposited in the office of the Surveyor-General, which was originally granted the   day of   , under the hand and seal of   Governor *(or Resident Commissioner)* of the said Province, to C. D., of *(insert description)*, in consideration of the sum of £   , paid to me by E. F., of *(here insert description)*, the receipt of which sum I hereby acknowledge, do hereby transfer to the said E. F. *(all my estate or interest, or a lesser estate or interest, describing such lesser estate)* in the said piece of land. In witness whereof I have hereunto subscribed my name this   day of   .

Signed on the day above named, by the said *A. B.*, in presence of *G. H.* }

C   SOUTH AUSTRALIA.

Lease.

I, *A. B.*, being seised of an estate *(here state nature of the estate or interest, whether in fee simple or life estate, or of a greater or less description than a life estate)*, subject, however, to such incumbrances, liens, and interests as are notified by memorandum endorsed hereon, in that piece of land situated in the *(County, Hundred or Township)*, of   , bounded on the *(here set forth boundaries in chains, links, or feet)*, containing *(here state area)*, be the same a little more or less *(exclusive of roads intersecting the same, if any)*, with right of way over *(here state rights of way, privileges, or easements intended to be conveyed)*, plan of which piece of land is delineated in *(margin hereof, or in map No.   , deposited in the Registry Office)*, which said piece of land is *(or is part of)*, the *(County, Section, or Town allotment)*, marked   , delineated in the public map of the said *(County, Hundred, or Township)*, deposited in the office of the Surveyor-General, which was originally granted the   day of   , under the hand and seal of   , Governor or Resident Commission of the said Province, to C. D. of *(insert description)*, do hereby lease to E. F. of *(here insert description)*, all the said lands, subject to the following covenants, conditions and restrictions *(here set forth all special covenants, if any, and state what covenants declared by "Real Property Act" to be implied against lessor and lessee respectively are intended to be barred or modified and in what manner)*, to be held by him, the said E. F., as tenant, for the space of   years, at the yearly rental of £   , payable *(here insert terms of payment of rent)*.

    I, E. F., of *(here insert description)*, do hereby accept this lease of the above described lands to be held by me, as tenant, for the term, and subject to the conditions, restrictions, and covenants above set forth.

Dated this   day of
    Signed by the above-named *A. B.* as lessor, and by the above-named *E. F.* as
lessee, this   day of   in presence of *X. Y.*
                        (Signed)

                                                    A. B. Lessor.
                                                    E. F. Lessee.

D   SOUTH AUSTRALIA.

Bill of Mortgage.
I, *A. B.*, being seised of an estate (*here state nature of the estate or interest, whether
in fee-simple or life estate, or of a greater or less description than a life estate*),
subject, however, to such incumbrances, liens, and interests as are notified by
memoranda endorsed hereon, in that piece of land situated in the (*County, Hundred, or Township*) of   , bounded on the (*here set forth boundaries, in
chains, links, or feet*), containing (*here state area*), be the same a little more or less
(*exclusive of roads intersecting the same, if any*) with right of way over (*here state
rights of ways, privileges, or easements appertaining*); plan of which piece of land
is delineated in (*margin hereof, or in Map No.   , deposited in the Registry
Office*), which said piece of land is (*or is part of*) the (*County, Section, or Town
allotment*) marked   , delineated in the public map of the said (*County, Hundred, or Township*), deposited in the office of the Surveyor-General, which was
originally granted the   day of   , under the hand and seal of
(*Governor or Resident Commissioner*) of the said Province, to *C. D.*, of (*insert
description.*)
    In consideration of the sum of £   , this day lent to me by *E. F.*, of (*here
insert description*), the receipt of which sum I hereby acknowledge, do hereby
covenant with the said *E. F.* that I will pay to him, the said *E. F.*, the above sum of
£   , on the   day of   : Secondly, that I will pay interest on
the said sum at the rate of £   by the £100, in the year, by equal payments,
on the   day of   , and on the   day of   , in every
year: Thirdly (*here set forth special covenants, of any are intended, and state
what covenants declared by "Real Property Act" to be implied in mortgages are
intended to be barred or modified; and if so, in what manner.*) And for the better
securing to the said *E. F.*, the repayment in manner aforesaid of the said principal
sum and interest, I hereby mortgage to the said *E. F.* all my estate and interest in
the said land above described.
    In witness whereof, I have hereto signed my name this   day of
        A. B., mortgagor.   Accepted, *E. F.*, mortgagee.
    Signed by the above-named *A. B.* as mortgagor, and by the above-named *E. F.*
as mortgagee, this   day of   in presence of *G. H.*

E   SOUTH AUSTRALIA.

Bill of Encumbrance.
I, *A. B.*, being seised of an estate (*here state nature of the estate or interest, whether

in fee simple or life estate, or of a greater or less description than a life estate), subject, however, to such encumbrances, liens, and interests, as are notified by memoranda endorsed hereon, in that piece of land situated in the *(County, Hundred, or Township)* of   , bounded on the *(here set forth the boundaries in chains, links, or feet)*, containing *(here state the area)*, be the same a little more or less, *(exclusive of roads intersecting the same, if any)*, with rights of way over *(here state rights of way, privileges, or easements appertaining)*, plan of which piece of land is delineated in *(margin hereof, or in map, No.*   , *deposited in the Registry Office)* which said piece of land is *(or is part of)* the *(County, Section, or Town allotment)* marked   , delineated in the public map of the said *(County, Hundred, or Township)* deposited in the office of the Surveyor-General, which was originally granted the   day of   under the hand and seal of   , Governor *(or Resident Commissioner)* of the said Province, to C. D., of *(insert description)*, and desiring to render the said land available for the purpose of securing to and for the use and benefit of E. F., *(here state the particulars of the annuity or sum of money desired to be secured, the times when, and the restrictions, limitations, conditions, and contingencies under which it is to be payable, and the particulars of any reversions or remainders desired to be secured or appointed)*, Do therefore set over and appoint all my estate in the said land to be encumbered to the extent and liable for the payment of the above specified sums in manner and subject to the conditions, restrictions, and contingencies, reversions, and remainders above specified.

In witness whereof I have hereunto subscribed my name this   day of
(Signed)   A. B.
Signed by the above-named A. B., in the presence of X. Y.

F   SOUTH AUSTRALIA.

Bill of Trust.

I, A. B., being seised of an estate *(here state nature of the estate or interest, whether in fee simple or life estate, or of a greater or less description than a life estate)*, subject, however, to such encumbrances, liens, and interests, as are notified by memorandum endorsed hereon, in that piece of land situated in the *(County, Hundred, or Township)* of   , bounded on the *(here set forth boundaries, in chains, links, or feet)*, containing *(here state area)*, be the same a little more or less *(exclusive of roads intersecting the same, if any)*, with right of way over *(here state rights of way, privileges, or easements appertaining)*; plan of which piece of land is delineated in *(margin, or in map No.*   , *deposited in the Registry Office)*. Which said piece of land is *(or is part of)* the *(Country Section, or Town allotment)*, marked   , delineated in the public map of the said *(County, Hundred, or Township)*, deposited in the office of the Surveyor-General, which was originally granted the   , day of   , under the hand and seal of   Governor *(or Resident Commissioner)* of the said Province to C. D., of *(insert description)*, desire to invest all my estate and interest in the above described land *(or a lesser estate in the said lands, specifying the nature and limitations of such lesser estate and all conditions, restrictions, limitations, and contingencies, rever-*

sions, and remainders, to which it is desired to subject the same) in trust for the uses and benefit of *C. D.* of   , and do therefore transfer, set over, and appoint all my estate and interest in the said lands *(or so much of my estate and interest in the same as is above limited and specified)* to *E. F.* and *G. H.* as trustees, to have and to hold the said estate and interest, in trust, for the uses and benefit of the said *C. D.*, subject to the conditions, limitations, restrictions, and contingencies, reversions, and remainders above set forth and specified.

In witness whereof I have hereunto subscribed my name and affixed my seal, this   day of   *A. B.*

I accept the above trust *E. F., G. H.*

Signed by the above-named *A. B.* as proprietor, and by the above-named *E. F.* and *G. H.* as trustees, this   day of   in presence of *X. Y.*

G   SOUTH AUSTRALIA.

Power of Attorney.

I, *A. B.*, being seised of an estate *(here state nature of the estate or interest, whether in fee simple or life estate, or of a greater or less description than a life estate)*, subject, however, to such incumbrances, liens, and interests as are notified by memorandum endorsed hereon, in that piece of land situated in the *(County, Hundred, or Township)*, of   , bounded on the *(here set forth boundaries in chains, links, or feet)*, containing *(here state area)*, be the same a little more or less *(exclusive of roads intersecting the same, if any)*, with right of way over *(here state rights of way, privileges, or easements appertaining)*, plan of which piece of land is delineated in *(margin hereof, or in map No.   , deposited in the Registry Office)*, which said piece of land is *(or is part of)*, the *(Country Section, or Town allotment)*, marked   , delineated in the public map of the said *(County, Hundred, or Township)*, deposited in the office of the Surveyor-General, which was originally granted the   day of   , under the hand and seal of   , Governor *(or Resident Commissioner)* of the said Province, to *C. D.* of *(insert description)*, do hereby appoint *C. D.*, attorney, on my behalf to *(here state the nature and extent of the powers intended to be conferred, as whether to sell, lease, mortgage, &c.)*, the above described lands *(or my estate and interest in the above described lands)*, subject, nevertheless, to the restrictions and limitations declared and set forth at foot hereof, and to execute all such instruments, and do all such acts, matters, and things as may be necessary for carrying out the powers hereby given, and for the recovery of all rents and sums of money that may become or are now due or owing to me in respect of the said lands, and for the enforcement of all contracts, covenants, or conditions binding upon any lessee or occupier of the said lands, or upon any other person in respect of the same and for the taking and maintaining possession of the said lands, and for protecting the same from waste, damage, or trespass.

I declare the above lands *(or my estate or interest in the above lands)*, shall not be sold for less than £   , or unless upon the following conditions *(here insert conditions, if any, to be imposed)*.

I declare the amount of money to be raised by mortgage on the security of the said lands under this power shall not exceed £   , or be less than £   ,

and that the rate of interest at which the same is raised shall not exceed £
for every £100 by the year.

I declare the above land shall not be leased for any term of years exceeding
, or at a less rent than £ , or unless subject to the following covenants and restrictions *(here insert conditions, such as whether right of purchase
may be given, and at what price, &c., &c.)*

I declare that this power shall not be exercised after the expiration of
from the date hereof.

In witness whereof I have hereunto subscribed my name this day of

Signed by the above-named *A. B.,* this

day of in presence of *X. Y.*

H   SOUTH AUSTRALIA.

Registration Abstract.

I, *A. B.,* being seised of an estate *(here state nature of the estate or interest, whether
in fee simple or life estate, or of a greater or less description than a life estate),*
subject, however, to such encumbrances, liens, and interests, as are notified by
memoranda endorsed hereon, in that piece of land situated in the *(County, Hundred, or Township)* of , bounded on the *(here set forth the boundaries in
chains, links, or feet),* containing *(here state the area),* be the same a little more or
less, *(exclusive of roads intersecting the same, if any),* with rights of way over *(here
state rights of way, privileges, or easements intended or appertaining),* plan of
which piece of land is delineated in *(margin, or in map, No. , deposited in
the Registry Office),* which said piece of land is *(or is part of)* the *(Country Section,
or Town allotment)* marked , delineated in the public map of the said
(County, Hundred, or Township) deposited in the office of the Surveyor-General,
which was originally granted the day of under the hand and
seal of , Governor *(or Resident Commissioner)* of the said Province, to
C. D. of *(insert description),* request that a registration abstract of my title to the
said lands may be granted, enabling me to sell, lease, or otherwise deal with the
same at places without the limits of the said Province.

(Signed) *A. B.*

To the Registrar-General

Signed by the above-named *A. B.,* this day of in presence of *X. Y.*

I, , Registrar-General of the Province of South Australia, do hereby
certify that the above particulars relating to the above described land and to the
estate and interest therein of *A. B.,* whose signature is above subscribed are correct
as appears by entries recorded in the register book of the said Province, Fo.

vol. No Pursuant, therefore, to the above application and by virtue of
powers in me vested by Act of the Legislature of the said Province, intituled "The
Real Property Act." This registration abstract is issued for the purpose of enabling
the said *A. B.* to deal with the said lands at places without the limits of the said
Province.

This abstract shall continue in force from the date thereof to the day
of unless sooner delivered up.

In witness whereof, I have hereunto signed my name and append my seal this day of

Registrar-General.
Signed, sealed, and delivered, the   day of   in the presence of *X. Y.*

I   SOUTH AUSTRALIA.

Application for Lands to be brought under operation of Act No.   of
          I, *A. B.*, of   do declare (*that I am*), or (*on behalf of*
(L.S.) of   , *that he is*) seised in possession of an estate (*here state the description of estate, whether in fee-simple or a lesser estate, or as trustee, or held in trust for uses*) in all that piece of land situated in (*here state the situation*) bounded (*here state the boundaries, and the length of each line of boundary, in chains and links, or in feet*), containing (*here state area*), be the same a little more or less, (*exclusive of roads intersecting the same, if any*) with (*here state rights of way and other privileges or easements appertaining*), plan of which piece of land is (*delineated in margin hereof, or in map No.   deposited in the Registry Office*) which piece of land is (*the town allotment or country section, or is part of the town allotment or country section*) originally granted to   of   by land grant under the hand and seal of   formerly Governer or Resident Commissioner of the Province of South Australia. Dated the   day of   numbered   in the plan of the (*district, or township, or county*) of   as delineated on the public maps of the Province deposited in the Survey Office in Adelaide: And I do further declare, that I am not aware of any mortgage, encumbrance, or claim affecting the said lands, or that any person hath any claim, estate, or interest in the said lands, at law or in equity, in possession or in expectancy, other than is set forth and stated as follows, that is to say—(*here state particulars of all unsatisfied mortgages, encumbrances, claims, or interests, if any*)—and I make this solemn declaration conscientiously believing the same to be true.
          Dated at   this   day of   18
          Made and subscribed by the above-named   this   day of
in the presence of me   Registrar-General or Justice of the Peace.
          I, *A. B.*, the above declarant, do hereby apply to have the piece of land described in the above declaration brought under the operation of Act No.
of 18
          Dated at   this   day of   18

A. B.

Witness to signature—*C. D.*

J   SOUTH AUSTRALIA.

Notice of receipt of Application for Lands to be brought under operation of Act. No.   of   or for the registration of transmission.
          Whereas   of   hath made and subscribed a declaration
(L.S.) before (*Registrar-General or Justice of the Peace*) setting forth (*that he is, or on behalf of   that he is*) seised of an estate in (*here recite*

the particulars from declaration), and hath made application to have the said **lands** brought under the operation of Act of Council No.　　　of 18　　, intituled the Real Property Act: Notice is hereby given, that, unless within the space of　　　from the date hereof, caveat be lodged with me by some person having estate or interest in the said lands, or by some person duly authorized on behalf of a person having estate or interest therein, I will proceed, as by law directed, to bring the said piece of land under the operation of the said Act.

　　　Dated this　　　day of　　　at the Registry Office, Adelaide, South Australia.

　　　　　　　　　　　(Signed)　　　　　　　Registrar-General.

K

Warrant of Lands Titles Commissioners.

Whereas *A. B.*, of　　　hath, by application No.　　　, dated the day of　　　, requested that the lands therein described be brought under the operation of the Real Property Act, and the said application has been referred to us by the Registrar-General, we hereby direct that publication of same be made in the following manner, that is to say *(or we find no sufficient grounds to entitle him to be recognized as holding fee-simple estate in the said lands)*, and in case no caveat be received by the Registrar-General in respect to such lands on or before the　　　day of　　　, we direct the Registrar-General to take such steps as are by law directed for bringing such land under the operation of the said Act.

　　　　　　　　　　　R. S.,⎫
　　　　　　　　　　　　　 ⎬　Lands Titles Commissioners.
　　　　　　　　　　　L. M.,⎭

Dated this　　　day of　　　185 .

L

Caveat.

Take notice that I,　　　claiming estate or interest *(here state the nature of the estate or interest claimed and the grounds on which such claim is founded)* in lands described as *(here state particulars of description from declaration of Applicant)* in notice dated the　　　day of　　　advertising the same as land in respect to which claim has been made, to have the same brought under the operation of Act of Council No.　　　, of 18　, intituled the Real Property Act, do hereby forbid the bringing of the said lands under the operation of the said Act.

　　　　　　　　this　　　day of
　　　　　　Signed in my presence this　　　day of　　　at
　　　　To the Registrar-General of the Province of South Australia.

M

Notice of Lands brought under Act.

Whereas *A. B.*, of　　　, claiming to be seised of an estate, in the lands described at foot hereof, has applied to have the said lands brought under the operation of the Real Property Act, and such claim having been duly advertised in manner prescribed by the said Act, and no caveat in respect to the said lands having been received by me within the time for that purpose by the said Act limited: Now I,   of   , Registrar-General by virtue of powers by the said Act in me vested, do hereby declare the said lands to be lands brought under the operation of the said Act, from and after the date hereof.

Given under my hand the   day of   185   .

Registrar-General.

N

Declaration of Owner taking by Transmission.

I   of   declare that   the proprietor of [*here describe the property and state the nature of the estate or interest transmitted (died at   , in the   , having first duly made his will, dated the day of   , whereby he appointed me executor, and I proved his said will on the day of   in the Court of   ), or (died at   , in the   , on the   day of   intestate, and that letters of administration of his estate and effects were on the   day of   duly granted to me by the Court of   ;]* or we declare that *C. D.* the proprietor of (*here describe the property and state the nature of the estate or interest transmitted) was on the   day of   (duly adjudged a bankrupt), or (declared insolvent),* and that we were on the   day of   appointed assignees of the said *C. D.*, and we are by law entitled to be registered as proprietors of the said land (*or of his interest therein as above described;]* or [I declare that on the   day of   I intermarried with and am now the husband of *C. D.*, the proprietor of (*here describe property and estate or interest therein transmitted),* and I declare that on such marriage the interest of the said *C. D.* became by law vested in me, and that I am entitled to be registered as proprietor of the said land or of her interest in the said land. And I make this solemn declaration conscientiously believing the same to be true.

(Signed)

Dated at   the   day of   18   .

Made and subscribed by the above-named *A. B.*, in the presence of me.

(Signed)   (*Name of the Registrar or Justice of the Peace acting in and for   )*

O

Transfer of Mortgage, Lease, or Encumbrance to be on or endorsed on Original Mortgage, Bill of Encumbrance, or Lease.

I, the within-mentioned *C. D.*, in consideration of £   this day paid to me by *X. Y.*, of   , the receipt of which sum I do hereby acknowledge, hereby transfer to him the estate or interest in respect to which I am registered as Proprietor, as set forth and described in the within-written security, together with all my rights, powers, estate, and interest therein. In witness whereof I have hereunto subscribed my name, this   day of

      (L. S.)   *C. D.*

     Signed by the above-named *C. D.*, in the presence of *E. F.*
the   day of

P

Caveat forbidding registration of contract for dealing with estate or interest in futuro.

    To the Registrar-General of South Australia—
Take notice that I   claiming estate or interest *(here state the nature of the estate or interest claimed, and the grounds on which such claim is founded)* in *(here describe land)* forbid the registration of any memorandum of sale, or other instrument, made, signed, or executed by *(here insert name and address of person supposed to have made, or suspected of being about to make, such memorandum of sale or other instrument)* affecting the said land, until this caveat be by me, or by the order of the Supreme Court, or some Judge thereof, withdrawn. Dated this *(here insert date of caveat)* day of   18   .

Q   SOUTH AUSTRALIA.

Revocation Order.

I, *A. B.,* of   being seised of an estate *(here state nature of the estate, whether in fee simple or of a less description)* in all that piece of land *(here describe land)* hereby revoke the power of mortgaging *(or selling)* the said land given by me to   by a power of attorney dated the   day of

    In witness whereof, I have hereunto subscribed my name and affixed my seal, this   day of

        (L. S.)   *A. B.* of

    I, *M. N.,* Registrar-General, hereby certify that the above-named proprietor has executed this revocation order in manner above appearing.

          (Signed)   Registrar-General.

R

Certificate of Registrar-General, Justice of the Peace, &c., taking declaration of attesting witness.

Appeared before me, at   the   day of   *(C. D.),* of   , the attesting witness to this instrument, and acknowledged his signature to the same; and did further declare, that *A. B.,* the party executing the same, was personally known to him, the said *C. D.*; and that the signature of this said instrument is the hand-writing of the said *A. B.*

          (Signed)   Registrar-general, or J. P.

S

Certificate of Registrar-General, or Justice of the Peace, before whom instrument may have been executed by the parties thereto.

Appeared before me, at   the   day of   , A. B. of   ,
the party executing the within instrument, and did freely and voluntarily sign the same.

(Signed)   Registrar-General, or J. P.

T

Fees payable to the Registrar-General for the performance of the several acts, matters, and things herein specified.

	£	s.	d.
For the bringing land under the operation of this Act, to be paid to the Lands Titles Commissioners, as provided for by Sec. No. 11, over and above the cost of all advertisements herein prescribed, to be in such case published	1	0	0
Receipt and noting of Caveat	0	10	0
Registering Memorandum of Sale, Bill of Mortgage, Bill of Trust, or Encumbrance, or Lease	0	10	0
For registering Transfer of Mortgage or of Eucumbrance, or Release of Mortgage or Encumbrance, or the Transfer or Surrender of a Lease	0	5	0
Registering Declaration of Ownership taken by Transmission	0	10	0
For every Certificate of Title	1	0	0
For every Power of Attorney	0	15	0
For every Registration Abstract	0	15	0
For cancelling Power or Registration Abstract	0	5	0
For every Revocation Order	0	10	0
Provisional Certificate of Title	1	0	0
For every search	0	3	0

Including the printed forms for each case prescribed to be used by this Act or by any regulation made in accordance with this Act; 2s. 6d. extra to be charged for any such instrument drawn on parchment.